Inclusion Starts with U

SARAH TABET

PASSIONPRENEUR
PUBLISHING

Publishing information
Publishing, design, and production facilitated by Passionpreneur Publishing, A division of Passionpreneur Organization Pty Ltd, ABN: 48640637529

www.PassionpreneurPublishing.com
Melbourne, VIC | Australia

DEDICATION

To my lovely and supportive family who stood by me against all odds, to my wonderful friends (you know who you are), partner, and to all the amazing mentors I've had over the years and the diverse leaders I have worked with, I dedicate this book. You all have helped me in your own unique ways, inspired me with your words or actions to help open my eyes, made me brave and bold to pursue my passion and set a clearer direction and purpose to my journey—
the journey of a free mind and spirit, the journey of change.
To all those who believed in me, understood me and trusted my aspirations and abilities, I thank you, as this book is a result of your love and support! You will always be my tower of strength.

TESTIMONIALS

"Inclusion is about walking the talk, and it starts with every single one of us. Sarah Tabet's advice on how to build an inclusive culture is enriched by years of practical experience working as a Diversity & Inclusion leader within a large multinational, and her vision could neither be more relevant nor timely. This is a fantastic read for anyone looking to play their part in driving real change across their organization or in their personal lives."

Sonali Satpathy
VP Diversity, Inclusion & Well-Being
Global Human Resources
Schneider Electric

Inclusion starts with U takes the reader through a journey in the voice of its author Sarah Tabet, an outstanding HR leader who was introduced to diversity and inclusion at work. Sarah shares her story on driving inclusion in the workplace delving into a broader perspective on how everyone can play a role at making the world more inclusive, ensuring respect for diversity in all of its forms. Inclusion starts with U will leave you with practical tips and an understanding that diversity is not only a corporate or workplace issue but one that is about mindset, culture, where every individual can play a role so that we all can live in a an equal and inclusive society and world.

The book is designed to give insights based on a personal experience, which very few books on diversity and inclusive take a storytelling approach highlighting challenges and opportunities and practical tips that can be implemented all in one resource. Inclusion starts with U offers a unique lens and great insight into how diversity and inclusion can be extended as a shared vision and responsibility by all. It is an exceptional resource for those looking to build their inclusive leadership in an increasingly divided world.

Noha Hefny
Award Winning Humanitarian,
Entrepreneur and Corporate leader
(Senior Consultant at UN Women,
Co-founder She is Arab)

Sarah is someone that is genuine to her core, applies herself at work and life with great intensity and passion. She is someone who is respected and revered within HR and the D&I field and has developed a broad and deep understanding on the key issues, particularly surrounding culture and diversity within our region.

Sami Zouehid
Partner and Executive Search Professional

TABLE OF CONTENTS

ACKNOWLEDGMENTS

Writing this book would have not been possible without the help, guidance and support of many people. I am so grateful for all you have done. A special acknowledgement to my parents, brothers, friends and partner for enduring me throughout in addition to Moustafa Hamwi and the team of passionpreneur publishing for making all this come together.

1

YES, I ALSO THOUGHT DIVERSITY WAS ALL ABOUT WOMEN

If you are always trying to be normal, you will never know how amazing you can be.

—*Maya Angelou*

My story begins like the stories of many ambitious women born and raised in the Middle East who fall victim to social pressure. For those who have never experienced that kind of pressure, well, I can tell you it's tough.

In many cases that kind of pressure can redefine you, shape you, and destroy what is colorful, unique, and different in you all with the aim of blending you back into nice pastel colors that make you justly fit into society's display case. That social pressure, as harmless as it is intended to be, can sometimes torment you. It makes you question every decision, sensation, or instinct you get, which might be different from what is recognized as the social norm. Reality is, it would push you to demonstrate to yourself, your parents, extended family, and community that what you aspire for is just as standard and as "normal" as society's expectations of you, regardless of how miserable that might make you.

Well, for me it has always been that thing: regardless of my ambitions, my dreams, my achievements, or what I become in life, in society's eyes, it is not as important, good enough, or rewarding as being married, having kids, and raising a family. Having said that, I cannot but mention that even being surrounded by a loving, open-minded family who has always recognized my success and potential ambitions and treated me fairly and as an equal to my brothers at home, granted me access to the best education, and encouraged me to lean in and grab any development opportunity, did not keep away the remotest of all relatives, who would suddenly get interested and question, "What's next?" They would say, "Clock is ticking. When will you finally settle? When will it be enough for you?" Sometimes subtly through jokes, but at other times bluntly and boldly they would ask, "Why the hassle to aspire for more? Why the effort?"

Similarly, their common responses to my career achievements would be, "Amazing. Congrats. That is great, but when will you focus on your personal life, on the true achievements in life? The more important things that matter, marriage and kids?" These are the statements that I would come across all the time from people hovering over my head, more so on my parents' heads.

Their expectations always seemed to be defined and clear. An ideal life for a girl: opt to find a decent job with decent working hours, marry the right guy, and find that happy ending to every story of a girl's life. It was not just one sentence that was said to me by someone, which changed my life, but the same sentence was told repeatedly so many times and for so many years that it transformed me. Many times I could not but think to myself, maybe they were right. Maybe I was not prioritizing well.

I would question myself, my ambitions, my dreams, my intuition and would scrutinize that fire I felt burning inside of me and pushing me to do more, not only as a professional in the corporate world, but also develop further as an individual. I would question every aspect of it and wonder why "normal" doesn't feel the same for me. Why am I different? Why do I feel different, and why couldn't I just feel as excited about the same things that make many others feel thrilled?

It was like no one understood what I truly aspired for, what kept me awake at night, and what brought me a sense of fulfillment. As much as I believed and aimed to achieve work-life harmony, create a balance between my personal and professional life, seek to settle with a partner who supported my journey, and start a family with whom I could share my successes, society's expectations were always different.

They expected that I define myself solely by motherhood, marriage, and based on my socially conditioned sense of duties. As it happens, while so much has changed in this world since the first movement of women and the call for equality in 1867—yes, 1867—still, in many regions, the perception of women remains quite the same, and professional success remains a second choice and a nice to have.

All encounters, events, and comments I faced throughout my journey—as insignificant and seemingly harmless as they might be—have truly changed me. In many instances, I stopped talking about my success, and if anything, I shyly shared my achievements. I stopped even telling people about my career aspirations or successes or progression and suppressed any feeling of excitement I had for new opportunities and plans. I acted indifferently. I convinced myself to slow down and thought of how to please others and align with their expectations. I tried even being interested in the discussions that other people considered normal for a lady of my age and within my community, and sometimes I made those choices that made everyone happy. Everyone but not me.

At other times I tried fighting back. I tried convincing people about my own view of life, my distinct aspirations, and my ambitions to fly high while leading both a successful professional life and with the right partner, an equally fruitful personal life. Yet people never bought it. "You are too ambitious," they said. "You will never find that kind of partner. Your dreams are too big. Continue on that route and you will find yourself alone."

All that scared me. I felt invaded, frustrated, as if people were defining my life and dictating what should make me happy and what won't. Well, to make life easier, I allowed people to influence and determine my choices sometimes. At other times, I pleased their expectations and acknowledged that the easier route was to act normal and do what people expected, regardless of the mental frustration or discomfort that it brought me.

For every decision I made I feared the possible impact and regret for not taking that normal route, that same safe train which everyone rode. It felt like I was constantly living someone else's life, a lie and act, hoping that nothing exciting would come my way—a new opportunity, a thrilling idea, or a choice to make—that would ultimately expose that act, disclose my true and unique self to others, and push me to embrace my differences and act upon them.

That act kept on going for years, creating in me that internal, bitter dispute between my mind and my heart. I kept on constantly fighting the worst battle between what I knew and what I felt. Between wanting to stay in that comfort zone or break that ceiling, embark on a new journey, the journey of freedom, freedom from that social pressure, and from what was considered the norm.

It was only when a new opportunity came up in 2017, an inspiring conversation about a possible radical change to my life—a career upgrade, a personal adventure—that everything changed. It made my eyes gleam, my heart beat, and my mind was set to dream again. That for me was the call for endless possibilities and limitless opportunities to discover and reinvent myself.

In July 2017, I moved from Lebanon to Dubai to expand my horizon as a human resources professional, a peoples' advocate, and a coach in the corporate world. With that move, I was fortunate enough to encounter professionals and counselors who played and still are playing active roles in highlighting the topic of women, specifically those from the Middle East, within both the corporate and social contexts. Those who live in the UAE know that every year this country hosts more than a thousand conferences, seminars, and roundtables to discuss different topics with more than 10% covering topics related to women. So, it is clear that the topic of women empowerment and gender equality has really become the talk of the hour and has been actively pursued across. Women are way better off than they were a hundred years ago and are better off today than they were fifteen years ago. Particularly in the Middle East, and with my HR access to job fairs and the job market, I have really seen more women earning educational degrees, graduating with MBAs, and becoming more ambitious to prove themselves in the corporate world and become economically self-reliant.

Generally speaking, yes, a lot of women have a lot more access to rights and opportunities such as education, work options, and reproductive health. In some countries, many women have been elected to parliament and many have held C-suite positions and are much more present in executive roles; but all in all, adding it all up, unfortunately, disparities still abound.

In the forums I have personally attended, I have listened to amazing women talk about their stories of surviving and growing their careers in tough environments, like the hospitality sector and financial institutions. I have met women who have struggled to promote themselves as leaders and fought to take seats at the table and be listened to in meetings. Many even had personal struggles to prove themselves as equal partners at home with equal career aspirations.

One story that touched me, and would have surely moved you, is the story of Eilyn. I can never forget Eilyn, that courageous lady who raised her hand and stood in front of five hundred women leaders who were discussing the need to break the ceiling to distinctly ask, "How can I convince my husband to 'let' me work?"

Did you know that in 2020, and as per the UN, in eighteen countries around the world, women are still not allowed to get a job without the permission of a male family friend or family member?

Did you know that in thirty-two countries, women still need permission to apply for a passport?

Did you know that in four countries, women are still not allowed to register a business?

Well, I did not know, but I cannot say that it did not shake me. It did. It unsettled me; it concerned me and made me think about how unfair this world still is. Eilyn's story, in addition to many others, has changed my world, my perspective, and my drive. They incentivized me to passionately change the perception of the world for all women who sought to grow, develop, and aim high, especially for those who believed they can do that and succeed professionally and personally side by side.

Those stories resonated with every negative or judging comment I personally got about being different; "too career oriented," "too independent," or even "too ambitious." Not only that, but it also made me decide then and there not only to call for women rights or talk about women empowerment, women leadership, or gender equality, but to fight for a bigger cause. To fight for a world of equality, a world of "Diversity and Inclusion" (D&I).

Diversity tends to be defined simply as a conglomeration of people from different backgrounds. The range of human differences, the state of quality or quality of being different. It touches every aspect of society and brings in the right mix of diverse genders, cultures, ethnicities, generation, work lifestyles, backgrounds, ages, disability, sexual orientation, communication, mindset, and much more.

While the term "Diversity" describes that mix, there are widespread research and unlimited examples of evidence-based practices confirming that that mix will only become "right" with the integration of "Inclusion." It is like a mixed salad with each person representing a distinct vegetable, be it a crisp carrot, a vibrant beet, or a lush romaine lettuce. Magic will only occur when that salad is doused with a dressing and all flavors become one—lemon mustard, ranch, or a light balsamic vinaigrette. That dressing of choice masks the very essence of Diversity and Inclusion and helps build that sense of belonging, purpose, and value for all kinds of diversities.

This is what we call Inclusion. Both Diversity and Inclusion have been seen as a critical factor in creating that melting-pot recipe of great ideas, thoughts, and perspectives. For me, though, driving Diversity and Inclusion developed to become really something deeper. It was a call for change. A determination to invest in building an inclusive workplace and a society that respects differences and values uniqueness. A world that promotes belonging and purpose for everyone, a fair and an equal world.

Through Diversity and Inclusion, I sought to promote equality, create awareness on what Inclusion is, help avoid discrimination and conflict, develop personal and professional relationships, and allow people to learn from each other. Beyond that, and more selfishly, I saw an opportunity to share with the world what took me some time to understand that "If you are always trying to be normal, you will never know how amazing you can be."

With this in mind, my journey began. I researched; I read; I connected with people with similar interests, be it on LinkedIn or at conferences; I investigated even in the workplaces by discussing with managers the need for diversity within their teams, the possible results of having teams with different backgrounds, nationalities, experiences and surely the impact of that on their businesses.

My understanding was mainly boosted by the extensive research that has been made over the past few years to recognize the importance of diversity as a foundation of creativity, and the significance of building an innovative culture to deliver a new business value. As I understood Diversity and Inclusion and talked about it in the corporate world and socially, I realized how many stereotypes have been built around it. Both Diversity and Inclusion have been made into buzzwords and catchy slogans, but unfortunately the phrase has been overused so many times that it has lost its true meaning.

For many people and organizations, the Diversity and Inclusion agenda simply stated the need to bring a woman's or maybe a person of color's perspective to the table; it is needless to mention the many people I know who thought that it was mostly about increasing the number of women in the workplace, which some have supported but others do not care much about. I was repeatedly asked by friends, especially in the corporate world, about the real need for the big fuss around gender balance in a world where women have indeed been offered many opportunities without question. In some instances, as a justification for driving diversity, some men even felt the need to a HeForHe campaign, instead of a HeForShe one supported by the UN on International Women's Day to claim against racism and sexism, which was being witnessed at many levels, especially on the hiring front.

At that moment I realized how much business leaders, HR professionals, and individuals at all levels and from every corner of this world did not truly understand this call for Diversity and Inclusion and it was my mission to step in. I had to clarify that D&I is not only for the corporate world; it's not only about me or only about you; it's really about all of us, and it can touch all our lives in all aspects. Imagine how you would feel as a parent if you are judged every time you leave work to pick up your kids or if you are expected to do more at work because you are single or have no children. Imagine how would you feel when people assume that as you get older, you will have no ambitions and no relevant skills or what would they say if they knew about your stress-related illness, panic attacks or burn-outs. Inclusion is all about that. Inclusion is the feeling that we all create to contribute to a better world, a world that respects differences and promotes belonging. A world where you and me can feel safe and secure and be who we really are and use our differences to achieve greatness. This is a feeling I have craved for when I felt alone in a world that does not understand my ambitions, and this is why *Inclusion Starts with I U*.

In the past few years, Diversity and Inclusion has become one of the biggest sound bites in the corporate speak, and as a passionate ambassador myself, I started leading this agenda across the Middle East and Africa in an organization that is fully committed to building and spreading a culture of inclusion to all diversities. Every day for me became, and still is, a new window for change, an opportunity to reform policies, and ensure inclusiveness to influence a change in mindset, to distinguish and combat bias, and a way for the transformation of strategy, priorities, and promoting inclusive environments.

I have worked extensively to lead this D&I transformation journey internally within the organization and externally as a strong advocate. As a result of my commitment,

I have been recognized as a speaker on this topic at several forums across the Gulf region. My articles have been featured in the *FBC Insights* in April 2018, *Siliconindia* in April 2019 issue, and I have been honored with the Women Leadership Excellence award for the category of Diversity and Inclusion in January 2020 by the MICE Quotient.

This reflects the work I have done and still do to spread the word around Diversity and Inclusion. I have learned not to listen to people who say my dreams are impossible, but rather have worked to prove them wrong.

The journey of influence and change is not easy, I must say. Throughout this journey, I met people who were ready to listen, craving to make that change within their organizations and communities, but also others who just couldn't relate. Because I've always been driven by passion and purpose, that did not stop me. I cannot deny though that sometimes those small acts of recognition that people showed also played an important role in helping me move the dial on D&I even further. At one of the events I spoke in October 2019, I was extremely thankful and happy to see this small note written by one of the attendees, who kept it on my seat. It said, "Thank you, Sarah, for sharing with us your experience and giving us valuable and inspiring advice; great speech, superb energy, and invaluable contribution. Keep inspiring, Lydia."

This note was so valuable to me personally as it reminded me then and there of my contributions to others, boosted my energy even further than what Lydia described, and just inspired me to keep going; therefore, *Inclusion Starts with I U*. I wrote this book for Lydia, Eilyn, and everyone else as a call for change, to realize my ambition to help individuals understand the true term of Diversity and Inclusion, and encourage them to join the conversation. It supports my intention to promote the importance of the D&I philosophy to business leaders and professionals, support them in delivering solutions, build a culture of inclusion in their organization, and encourage all forms of diversities that will help deliver new business value, maximize human capital, and help build an equal and enabled world.

Now that you know how D&I relates to me, in the next chapter and as a start, I will be sharing some additional insights on the book *Inclusion Starts with I U*, exposing some forms of exclusions that need to be addressed, and shed light on the pillars of my PBM system to help address those.

2

OPERATION EARTHQUAKE

We need more rebels!

George Dei says, "Inclusion is not about bringing people into what already exists. It is really making a new space, a better space for everyone."

With regard to the space we live in, I'm sure we can see significant efforts made by governments, corporations, schools, communities, and many others in supporting the integration and inclusion of diverse individuals with diverse needs. But is it enough? Inconsistencies, unfortunately, still exist in the world we live in; misconceptions remain and efforts are still falling short of the mark.

In this chapter, I would be shedding light on the extended scope of Inclusion, share some of the remaining inconsistencies, and clarify why each and every one of us needs to be a rebel to exclusion, a leader of Operation Earthquake, regardless of our occupation, influence, and decision-making opportunities. By the end of this chapter, I will be sharing with you details about the PBM system to touch on the different aspects of Inclusion.

It is really fair and common to say that recently there has been an alphabet soup of terms focused on encouraging fairness around the world. Most governments and organizations have used terms such as equity, engagement, culture, belonging, and fairness, but the most common phrase is still Diversity and Inclusion or D&I.

The question always remains, are these concepts similar, complementary, or different? The truth is that too many organizations, public or private, still make the same mistake of assuming that Diversity and Inclusion are really synonyms or that one automatically implies the other, and that mistake is arguably a risky one.

A few months back I was intrigued and positively surprised to read an article written by my brother, David, about a topic very close to my heart, the topic of Diversity and Inclusion. This article was called, "Is It Time to Redesign for Inclusiveness?" My brother has been working in consultancy for many years, and he naturally developed a sense for solving problems and creating immediate strategies to address gaps and is really passionate about practically implementing changes.

In this article, David talks about one day, like many other days, of his life; his routine includes passing by a coffee shop in the morning on his way to the office, picking up a snack, placing it on the counter, paying for it, and continuing on to work. Only this time his experience was different. Having picked up the snack, he placed it on that counter and was kindly asked by the cashier to bring the snack closer, as he could not reach it. David then realized that the shop had hired a little person for whom the counter was simply too high.

Recognizing the positive efforts of many when it comes to the integration of differently abled people in everyday life like priority parking, seating, and incentivizing organizations to employ them, I can say that this has surely positively impacted the diversity aspect, but does that promote inclusion too?

Thinking about Jose, this cashier at the shop I mentioned, I couldn't but imagine how many times a day he must make the same kind of request to almost each and every customer almost at every encounter, hoping to be noticed and be supported to do his usual job. Aside from that hassle, of course, needless to mention the possible anxiety and discomfort when having to highlight his difference to every customer on a daily basis and accept possibly any unjustified judgment or reaction that might come with it.

It is at such moments that you realize how many things around us were not and are still not designed to encourage inclusion. Most coffee shop counters are too high for short people or for people on wheelchairs. Airport scanners are not made for people who have difficulties lifting luggage, such as elderly people, little people, pregnant women, or unaccompanied minors. Compartments in airplanes are too high to reach, and seats do not account for either large or very tall people.

We can go on and on about the small and big things around us that are just standardized across with absolutely no consideration for people's differences. As a result, differently abled individuals still experience increased dependency and restricted participation in their society, even in high-income countries.

To prove that, based on the World Report on Disability published by the WHO, 20% to 40% of people with disabilities still lack the help they require to engage in everyday activities. Accordingly, this social exclusion, as defined in sociology, leads to the disadvantage of human life and develops a poorer sense of well-being, inequality, poverty, and unemployment on many levels.

Considering the professional front and the workplaces we work in, exclusions are also still heavily felt and highlighted in different aspects. Recent studies made on twenty large US firms, surveying three thousand employees from mixes of ages, gender, seniority, ethnicities, and sexual orientation, found that 61% of employees report that they are covering their identity in some way or another in their organization. Although covering of identity was more prevalent among traditionally underrepresented groups, this surprising incidence was also highlighted among straight white men, 45% of whom mentioned that they downplayed characteristics such as age, physical disability, or mental health issues due to fear of judgment. This is a highlighted risk that is leading them to live as their diminished self, which can have powerful and negative consequences over time on them and on those around them.

Aside from the professional front, also on the personal front, I have also been hearing more and more about the "social costs" of being different. This refers to the impact of the social exclusion that can be connected to people's social class, race, skin color, religious affiliation, ethnic origin, educational status, and many, many more aspects. Basically, anyone who appears to deviate in any way from perceived norms of the population may become subject to the subtle form of social exclusion characterized as an exclusion form of discrimination and comes with that social cost.

As an example of that I would like to tell you about Joan. I met Joan recently at a social gathering, where we started discussing about my interest in the Diversity and Inclusion topic when, interestingly, she started describing how she started feeling more and more socially excluded just for the fact that she has turned vegan. Being vegan makes her feel isolated from people as she must constantly explain her veganism to everyone. Digging deeper, I understood that aside from the normal curiosity of people to understand how veganism works, she must constantly answer questions about why it is not wrong to be a vegan, and she is viciously, personally, and persistently attacked about her life choices. Her veganism becomes the focus of every conversation at every gathering, making her feel weird and judged just because she doesn't eat like everyone else. As a result of these experiences, her differences started isolating her, forcing her to retire from even bringing this topic up, and she realized how much people are not open to differences. If you are different, some people don't even want to talk to you because the normal topics don't apply to you. It's harder for them to relate, and this, by itself, generates a high social cost for you.

As Charles Evans Hughes says, "When we lose the right to be different, we lose the privilege to be free." To be free, we need to personally become more inclusive, rebel against exclusions we see within our societies and workplaces, and build a new and inclusive world. We all need to initiate Operation Earthquake, the operation that can drastically influence our mindset, make big disruptions in the world around us as we know it today, and just create an impact.

If we want to build that renewed inclusive world, we need to focus on three areas that I define as PBM: policies, behaviors, and mindsets. In this book, we will be talking about PBM within three contexts: professional, personal, and social, all with the aim of building Inclusion.

In the professional context, we will highlight the need to invest in Diversity and Inclusion and then share some tips on how to build inclusive workplaces through revising our policies and practices to help maximize human capital across organizations. On the personal front, we will be focusing on behavior and how understanding the three topics of inclusive leadership, women empowerment, and hidden biases are essential for our enhanced interaction with people. Finally, on the social front, we will also be reiterating the need to focus on a change in mindset, our need to learn to accept and value people's differences, and believe in our power to build an equal, inclusive-enabled world.

While Diversity and Inclusion has become a priority for some companies, governments, and international organizations, in this chapter I have discussed the wider scope of D&I to reinforce the need for us to push further on all levels—professionally, personally, and socially—and to redesign small, yet significant aspects of our daily routines to give everyone a better opportunity to be included.

In the next chapter, I will be focusing on the importance of Inclusion in the workplace and why both HR and business leaders need to invest in D&I to drive innovation and maximize business potential.

3

DIVERSITY IS AN ACTION, INCLUSIVITY IS A CULTURE

Change doesn't start from top-down leadership; it happens at all levels

Josh Bersin says, "Companies that embrace Diversity and Inclusion in all aspects of their business, statistically out-perform their peers." Yes, it might be true that most of us know intuitively that Diversity and Inclusion is good for the business and the strong moral argument that supports it, but the impact on the bottom line, as proven by several case studies, is even stronger. Whether you are a business leader, an HR professional, an entrepreneur, or a business person at any level, this chapter is for you.

In the past few years, Josh Bersin, a world-known industry analyst and founder of Bersin—a leading provider of research programs and human resources—has published articles and case studies that prove the impact of diversity on profitability, innovation, growth, engagement, and many other aspects that help maximize human capital.

In this chapter, I will be shedding light on some of those business realities and investments made in Diversity and Inclusion in the workplace and why this has proven to contribute to a better world and a more sustainable business.

If you want to be part of a successful revenue-generating business or lead one to growth, then invest in Diversity and Inclusion; that is key, and I will tell you why: A recent Harvard business school survey found that companies with more diversity in their teams made between 18% and 69% more than other companies in terms of net income and operating revenue. Meanwhile, businesses with a more gender diverse board saw a 42% higher return in sales, 66% greater return on invested capital, and 53% higher return on equity. As for the millennials, a generation that is expected to make up 75% of the workforce by 2025, that is five years from now, are demanding that organizations value and be intentional about Diversity and Inclusion in all its aspects.

Employees from this generation want their voices to be heard and their ideas to be considered. They want to feel safe to have a more open and transparent conversation and a more inclusive environment. So it is no secret that for your organization to thrive, you need to offer that. The public is going to judge you, and potential candidates are going to consider both the diversity of your workforce, and how welcoming your workplace is before even considering your job offer. While this might be demanding, it is also a good thing as everyone, finally, has gotten a bit more serious about the topic of Diversity and Inclusion. So, let's also get more serious ourselves and look at things we can initially do to kick off the workplace D&I journey.

While many believe that having a diverse and inclusive culture is critical to performance, it is not always clear to them how to achieve that goal. They don't know how to do it or what does it mean. So here are three powerful truths that can help this aspiration turn into reality.

1. **You must be intentional and serious about diversity**. While there is a good amount of data and research on the benefits of more diverse teams, progress in this area continues to move at a snail's pace. Although leaders are critical in moving the needle on diversity, change must happen at every level of the organization, and it must be influenced by everyone. Throughout my career in HR, I have experienced how much humans are attracted to similarity. This natural love of things that are similar to us is one of the most robust and consistent findings in psychology. And unfortunately, this impacts the way we look at Diversity and Inclusion. Research has shown that the love

of the same relates to different attributes such as race, gender, country of birth, nationality, language, background, and even things like wearing of glasses, hair length, and color.

This sense of identity attracts us to people who are like us, and then at the workplace it makes us want to work more, connect, develop, hire, even promote people similar to us. Interestingly enough, even professor Donn Byrne has published a research in 1992 that confirms that we are 260% more likely to contribute to a hurricane relief fund if the name of that hurricane starts with the same letters as our name. Yes, so it is our human nature to attract people who are like us, and probably, it is easier to connect to and work with those like-minded teams. However, knowing that diversity produces better results in the workplace, we need to challenge our human nature and put in that extra effort to attract, retain, develop, and promote more diverse teams, people who are different from us who will play an active role in taking diversity in the workplace to the next level.

2. It is important to **create that inclusive workplace**. Merely creating a diverse team won't automatically make that team successful. Inclusion is just as important. To be inclusive, it is crucial to generate a collaborative, supportive, and respectful environment to increase the participation and contribution of all employees. People feel included

only when they are treated fairly and with respect. This can apply to different aspects, but as a starting point it would be important to revisit all internal policies and the principles with attention to discrimination. A simple example on how our policies do not embrace differences today is in the way we celebrate our holidays in the workplace. For example, being in the UAE, a melting pot for expats from diverse nationalities, religions, beliefs, we tend to forget that people have different needs of celebrating different holidays. So instead of only mandating in our policies the official holidays set by the government based on country regulations, one step toward inclusion would be to provide flexibility in our policies to tolerate people's different needs, like celebrating Diwali, Christmas, or other important holidays based on the different religious calendars. Any initiative, though, taken on the corporate or personal level will only be successful if everyone experiences that feeling of belonging in the workplace where everyone's point of view, background, and personal needs are heard and taken into consideration.

3. **Provide psychological safety.** That next element means to feel valued and safe. Inclusion is practiced when people believe that their unique and authentic self is valued by others. It is expressed as a feeling of safety to speak up or show who you truly are or what you believe in without fear of

embarrassment or retaliation. To create that environment, we need to provide that psychological safety. It is the belief that no one will be punished or humiliated for speaking up and proposing new ideas, asking questions, raising concerns, giving feedback, or even making mistakes. It is about how we, in the workplace, react to the different ideas put on the table, possible unpopular views, or mistakes people have done or might do. How many times have you attended meetings, for example, where no one voiced their opinions, there was not much discussion, and people simply went along with what the manager has said for fear or judgment or risk of sticking their necks out and having it cut off?

This fear not only impacts people's engagement, motivation, and involvement, but obviously hinders innovation, creativity, and business growth. A recent research published by the *Harvard Business Review* (*HBR*) confirmed that psychological safety stood out as one of the most important factors for creating a successful team. Generating positive emotions like trust, curiosity, confidence, and inspiration broadens the mind and allows complex problem-solving and fosters cooperative relationships. When we feel safe, we become resilient, motivated, and persistent. So, there are three ways to foster that psychological safety at work:

1. Replace blame with curiosity. Adopt a learning mindset to understand what happened. Be

curious about what was missed, what can be done differently, and what could be the ideal scenario.

2. Encourage active listening, inspire people to share more, ask questions, and reconfirm that out-of-the-box ideas are encouraged.

3. Remind people you are different, just like them. People have beliefs, perspectives, and opinions, just like you. People have hopes, anxieties, and vulnerabilities, just like you. People have families, kids they love, parents they take care of just like you. Everyone wants to feel respected, recognized, and valued, just like you. If you start by creating this sense of psychological safety on your own teams as of now, you can expect to see high levels of engagement, increased motivation to tackle those difficult problems, and more learning and development opportunities, which lead to better performance.

To prove that, in 2018 and with the aim to tackle the reality of the D&I evolution across corporations, Deloitte shared an interesting story about Qantas, the Australian national carrier:

In 2013, Qantas posted a record loss of 2.8 billion Australian dollars, as reported in their annual report. This low point in the airline's ninety-eight-year history followed record-high fuel costs, the grounding of its A380s in 2010 for engine trouble, and the suspension of its entire fleet for three days in 2011 after a series of bitter union disputes. Across the country, forecasts about the fate of Australia's national carrier were terrible. Fast forward to 2017, Qantas delivered a record profit of 850 million Australian dollars, increased its operating margin to 12%, won the "world's safest airline" award, ranked as Australia's most trusted big business and its most attractive employer, and delivered shareholder return in the top quartile of its global airline peers. How did that happen?

CEO Alan Joyce answered, "We have a diverse environment and a very inclusive culture." According to Joyce, "Those characteristics got us through the tough times. Diversity generated better strategy, better risk management, better debate, and better outcomes." This is a real proof that Diversity and Inclusion works. Qantas is not the only company that has turned things around due to its Diversity and Inclusion strategy and has become very serious about this topic. There is considerable research by Boston Consulting Group, Deloitte, JP Morgan, McKinsey, MIT, and many others to show the advantages that Diversity and Inclusion brings to an organization, some of which are increased profitability and creativity and enhanced problem-solving. Employees with diverse experiences bring their own perspectives, ideas, skills, and practices to help create organizations that are resilient and effective, sensible to differences, accommodating, and open, which can help the organization outperform others.

To take that to the next level and succeed as a business, you need to acknowledge that while the benefits of creating a diverse, inclusive, and psychologically safe environment are plentiful, it is also a kind of investment in people and culture. It is a kind of relationship that needs to be practiced regularly and at all levels, an inclusive culture that needs to be cultivated daily. If you consider this as a one-time campaign or a one-off initiative, people will know, they will figure it out, they will realize that your initiatives might not be rooted in a real desire for change but are purely a public relations effort. Promoting Diversity and Inclusion in the workplace is a constant work in progress and therefore needs continuous nurturing.

It's important that you also recognize and reconfirm that investing in D&I is not a just feel-good move; it is really good for the business on all fronts. So, in this chapter we have seen how Diversity and Inclusion has been a real transformative force for some businesses leading to pre-eminent sustainability and growth but also how others might feel ill-equipped to navigate these swirling waters. To support them, we have examined some actions that can be followed to translate some of their intentions of investing in D&I into meaningful processes. What is worth mentioning here is that while some companies overemphasize on diversity, they sometimes underemphasize on inclusion and underestimate the depth of change that is required to ignite a true cultural reset that would drive positively people's performance and then the businesses'.

There is so much to learn, obviously, on Diversity and Inclusion in the workplace, but it is also important to remember that every company's initiative will look different. Diversity means different things to different people and Inclusion will be measured differently based on each organization's needs. Thus, for real change to happen, every individual from top to bottom of the pyramid needs to buy into the value of Diversity and Inclusion in the workplace, both intellectually and emotionally. So in summary, it is no secret that the intangible gains earned from such an investment, not to mention the financial impact, should put this subject high on your list and on every businessperson's priority list. It is a worthy business investment with strong returns, so make sure to bring it to the forefront of your business. This leads us to digging deeper into the next step of changes we need to make in the workplace to promote both Diversity and Inclusion. This is especially related to the policies we can create and implement. In the next chapter, we will be talking more about the topic of flexibility at work and the impact on the workplace culture.

4

FLEX @ WORK IS NOT THE FUTURE; IT IS THE PRESENT!

No, flexibility doesn't mean just working remotely

The world has changed. Men and women have completely different expectations of work, and yet, too often, systems and company policies and ways of work have not changed to allow for this. Over the past years, we have watched with great interest how remote working has gradually been drifting toward mainstream acceptance, but it was widespread only among early adopters, for those who worked in a specific set of sectors or industries, or those who chose to or could afford to accept it. It has been really difficult to draw universally acceptable arrangements and get the support of many, mostly employers, to see the benefit of that. Well, in one fell swoop, the novel coronavirus, COVID-19, changed all of that.

As I was writing this, millions of people around the world were ordered to self-quarantine and many were mandated by governments or employers to work remotely. Although many organizations did not consider this arrangement in the past and probably were not convinced about it, this epidemic, unexpected and unprecedented, has put remote work to a massive test and on a totally unique scale. People are on lockdown, schools are closed, universities have been put on hold, and many actions have been taken to control the spread of the virus. This has pushed everyone to account quickly and suddenly for the possible business impact and sustainability of their day-to-day operations and, most importantly, the needs of their employees in managing both their professional and personal responsibilities. This pivotal moment has forced masses of people to adjust to and accelerate the change.

In this chapter, we will discuss how remote working—not the only aspect of Flex @ work—has gained a lot of attention from organizations and scholars to become in today's world not only a luxury or a perk provided by companies to attract talent, but rather a way for business survival, a necessity, an integral part of the company's culture. Additionally, I will provide some tips on how to implement this in the workplace while considering both employee and employer challenges.

It is true that the coronavirus is probably an extreme example to show the importance of remote working and Flex @ work arrangement in today's world, but don't you think that these arrangements can also be great for long-term productivity, critical for people's engagement, and essential in boosting inclusiveness? To help you reflect on this, maybe as a first step, it is worth clarifying the scope of what is Flex @ work: In today's definition, many think of it as the umbrella term used to describe any role that breaks the traditional norm of a rigid 9 to 5, five-day-week structure. It is an approach that gives potentially greater freedom over when, where, or how individuals can fulfill their particular roles while delivering the same or better results to the organization. The term also covers all types of part-time work, compressed hours, flex time, remote working, break arrangements, casual dress, telecommuting, caregiving leaves, and many others.

Flex @ work has been linked to job satisfaction, engagement, motivation of employees in addition to cost effectiveness for employers. Although stereotypically we know that when we think about flexible work, often we think of a woman who is trying to balance parenting responsibilities with her paid job, nevertheless, research shows that flexible work doesn't address just maternal issues, but rather offers numerous benefits to both employers and employees. Such benefits can include:

- Widening the pool of talent by offering flexible working patterns, especially for hard-to-fill roles. It would support attracting the new generation and providing global access to global talent pool.

- It can also enhance the morale of workers by creating the work–life balance they need.
- It could improve retention of good performers and top talent who are looking for the new, smart ways of working.
- It will boost productivity due to the loss of pointless daily commuting time from and to the office.
- It will impact engagement positively and increase the motivation of employees who feel their needs are listened to and want to give back to that organization.
- It would minimize the harmful impact on the environment by contributing to sustainability efforts by reducing carbon emissions and workplace footprints in terms of creating of new office buildings, and that would in turn reduce the cost of desk space.

So as an employer, there are endless positive reasons to look into Flex @ work. I understand there could be trust issues, but as an employer, if you trust people to get their work done in ways that work for them, that trust is usually rewarded. Believe it or not, when it comes to employee motivation, money isn't anymore as important as you might think. Today more than ever before, everyone is looking to be part of something bigger—bigger than themselves—their career progression or the need to compete with their peers for the next best role. People want to work for a purpose; they want to positively impact something or someone while enjoying a good work–life balance. They want to be able to check the status of an important project while waiting to catch a flight or replying to a coworker's e-mail from their favorite cafe. They want to be able to shift their working hours to make time to take an aging parent to a doctor's visit or pick up their children from the nursery when needed. Each of these scenarios and personal preferences has one thing in common: they are made possible through Flex @ work.

This arrangement is not anymore a reflection of the future of work but has become really the reality of our present. It is critical for businesses to understand the importance of promoting Diversity and Inclusion through Flex @work and its impact on their business results. It is, however, also important to consider that workplace flexibility is more than only giving people a flexible schedule or a work from home option to best suit their needs; there are six other aspects that we can contemplate:

1. Flexible arrival and departure times: this provides freedom to change work schedules from one week to the next depending on the employee's personal needs. This, however, will specify required standard core hours where everyone will be connected.
2. Full-time or part-time work from home or location flexibility: this can be applied for jobs that require independent work, little face-to-face interactions, concentration, and a measurable and results-based

work product instead of a time-based deliverable. In many jobs, physical location has become less important than the efficiency of operations.

3. Part-time jobs: these are offered to attract a workforce that includes students, parents of young children, older generation, highly technical experts, and others who need or want to work but do not wish to work on a full-time schedule. This can help build a pipeline for organizations and retain professionals who otherwise would be lost.

4. Compressed shifts or work week: this provides freedom to implement a four-day work week of ten hours a day, for example. Employers would get the same number of working hours, but employees will have a three-day weekend every week. This arrangement usually helps employees whose family status involves childcare or elder-care responsibilities and may give them particular value in saving time and commuting expenses.

5. Opportunity for sabbatical or career breaks: this is considered a winning idea to help people feel rejuvenated, recharged, and inspired to work with renewed energy and focus.

6. Caregiving leave: this provides flexibility for people to take time away from work to provide care or support to a critically ill or injured family member which is not usually covered on the typical paid leave entitlement. This arrangement will be

> covered and discussed in more detail in the coming chapters.

So, all in all, some companies have implemented improved policies that consist of different types of flexible arrangements that people can use either in combination or separately to empower them to live and work in a way that works best for them. Finally, these policies have started to become a universally acceptable working style and no longer a faux pas.

According to research and based on the employee job satisfaction engagement reports from the SHRM, 55% of employees cited that Flex @ work is a very important aspect of their job satisfaction. It has been considered as one of the top reasons employees would be unlikely or very likely to look for new positions outside of their organization. It has been surging in popularity across countries and generations. The same research confirms that 92% of millennials identify flexibility as a top priority when job hunting, 80% of women and 52% of men want that flexibility in their next role, and most over the age of fifty want to ease into retirement through reducing hours and working flexibly. As an answer to the pleas, it is encouraging to see that based on the 2019 Deloitte survey that questioned 13,416 millennials (born between 1983 and 1994), many have been benefiting from the adoption of Flex @ work and its different arrangements:

69%
Flexible Time
Employees choosing
when they
start/finish work

68%
Flexible Role
Employees choosing
within certain
guidelines, what
they do as part of
their job

67%
Flexible
Recruitment
Offering different
types of contracts,
crowd-sourcing
talent, etc.

64%
Flexible Location
Employees choosing
to work from the
office, from home
or other locations

Source: https://www2.deloitte.com/global/en/pages/about-deloitte/articles/millennialsurvey.html

Similarly, if you think about yourself and your own personal obligations and family responsibilities, how many times have you wished to make that important parent–teacher conference during the day or needed to go back to school to pick up your kid or simply be home when the technician needed to come to fix your air conditioner? How many times have you wished you could exercise in the morning and compensate for that work at night or focus a bit more on exercising this hobby you have stopped doing or passion you have been ignoring? I know I have, and you too, being an employee or employer, can appreciate that flexibility, all without having to neglect work in favor of any personal responsibilities.

Despite its numerous proven advantages, for any flexible working policy to take hold and to be truly hardwired into the organization, it requires a huge change in culture. It is essential that initially it is role-modeled by leaders who understand and acknowledge its challenges in parallel to its advantages. For some employees, Flex @ work still can be perceived as negatively impacting their career advancement as they might be seen unavailable if away from the hub activities, office politics, management, and flow of information. From the employer standpoint, still, many do not support that arrangement because of lack of trust. In order to mitigate that, it is essential not only to invest in the new technology that allows digital communication and collaboration, but also lead a shift in culture across the board to mandate less regulation and more trust in people. This is when it is worth reminding managers that since we place our trust in employees from the moment they start working with us, why wouldn't that same theory apply when it comes to flexibility? If you trust someone enough to hire them, you should also trust them to get the work done when and where they prefer as long as they meet the deadline. To support that, extra efforts need to be made in establishing set expectations among all and create unique methods of evaluation to lead from distance.

It is fair to say that many people don't want to spend their whole lives at work anymore. Instead, they look for opportunities to spend time with their loved ones, family, friends, and pets or really partake in their hobbies. Therefore, giving them the ability to balance their lives is really an investment, an investment in people and business. It is true that some businesses have been slower than others in embracing this change, whether out of fear or ignorance, irrelevance or complexity, but many have realized the opportunities that Flex @ work brings to the business and to the people. Many who have adopted it, willingly or mandatorily, due to unexpected circumstances like the COVID, know that the sky hasn't fallen since they allowed it. Teams have been as productive, clients have been equally supported, and operations have been mostly seamless. Employees have been overwhelmingly positive and supportive of the change in culture and in the ways of working.

Therefore, given the present and future of work and the need to ensure that inclusive environment, we are reminded to create that culture of Flex @ work where everyone— men, women, parents, and non-parents—would feel equally entitled to achieve the work–life balance they need. It is hugely important in today's society that we are supportive of every family situation and respect people's responsibilities on both professional and personal aspects. As more people adopt flexible work, the emphasis would naturally shift to the quality of people's work and what they are delivering to the business rather than the hours they spend at their desks. This is good not just for the feeling of inclusion and engagement of people, but also for business productivity and cost efficiency. Flexibility needs to be more than just a policy; it should be a working culture that accommodates employees' changing needs and more of a company's investment in the future.

If we look at the bigger picture and the overall cultural change and call for Diversity and Inclusion in the workplace, I believe that if we are ever going to achieve gender equality; increase the number of female leaders, executives, and board members; and remove the negative stigma attached to males asking for more flexibility to take on more domestic roles, flexibility must be openly and unreservedly available to all employees. As a flexible working ambassador myself, I advocate for flexibility to become imperative to creating a diverse and inclusive workplace and ask you to start considering Flex @ work as the evolution to a new normal life. There is no question that Flex @ work policy is a critical enabler in retaining talent within any organization and making workplaces more inclusive, but it is equally critical to look at all our policies to ensure they become more family friendly and account for the diverse needs of diverse people in today's world. In the next chapter, we will be dwelling more on the topic of family-friendly policies and how those too can help promote Diversity and Inclusion in the workplace.

5

IF YOU CARE ABOUT ME, CARE ABOUT MY FAMILY

Did you know that companies compete annually to gain a coveted place on the list of top employers for working families?

It is no secret that now more than ever employers are looking at ways to make themselves stand out from the crowd so that they can win and keep talent, increase employee engagement and satisfaction, and see that employees thrive and support the growth of the business.

Employee satisfaction is about many things, but for parents and caregivers, the ability to positively reconcile work and family life remains high on their priority list. This can be achieved not only through Flex @ work policies which we covered earlier, but also through family-friendly policies that can support their needs and lifestyle.

In our modern days, there is no "traditional" when it comes to families anymore. It has become critical to understand and embrace the broader definition of family, which could include single parents, same-sex couples and unmarried couples, stepparents, extended family members, and other diverse forms that make traditional concepts and policies in companies harder to register. Therefore, it is important that family-friendly policies be embedded in our organizations to help benefit both work and family life and demonstrate commitment to Diversity and Inclusion.

In this chapter, we will be learning about the different family-friendly policies that can be incorporated and the different possible family considerations to account for when revising our policies.

Two years ago, Amy, a young top talent employee who recently got promoted, asked to meet with me formally. Considering my role as an HR leader, I did not see that unusual of course, but the anxiety and discomfort I noticed on her face when she came into my office was quite unusual. While I was trying to understand her concern, Amy started sharing her story about how she and her husband Tom have been struggling with infertility since they got married and finally made the decision to adopt a child. Being American citizens, they had already contacted foster care centers in the United States and were ready to travel to complete the necessary documentation and legal process there and come back to the Middle East with the baby they had been waiting for. As much as I knew Amy was excited about the whole experience, she was equally anxious about the logistics and details that followed.

Amy looked at me with despair and said, "I have been going through our policies and realized that adoption is not covered under maternity entitlement, nor mentioned as a right for employees. So how am I expected to adopt a child and be back at office the next day? I have no support here, no one to take care of my child, and I cannot even imagine the idea of enrolling him in daycare only after few days of his adoption. Not to mention that Tom is also only entitled for five days of paternity leave, which isn't even enough for us to complete the documentation and be back on time. I think this is unfair and inconsiderate, and has pushed me to submit my resignation. As much as I love this organization, I would always put my family first."

Much to my surprise and disappointment, I knew Amy was right. Our policies were very traditional; they were inconsiderate and completely exclusive. Like many organizations, our maternity policies covered only birth mothers, paternity leave was limited to a few days only, and our general leave policies were standard and simply not inclusive.

How many Amys do you know who are willing to throw away years of success, investment in their development, and possible bright careers in order to meet their family needs? I know many. What I also know is that nowadays the only way to attract, engage, and retain the Amys of this world within our organizations is by revising our policies to become more family-friendly and more humane.

So here are five ways businesses can help create more family-friendly policies and workplaces:

1. Revise the definition of family: Too often in our policies, we define family narrowly based on an outdated concept of a married husband, wife, and their biological children. Reality is that many families have long departed from that nuclear model and shifted into a less-traditional setup. Step-this and half-that not only has become a bit outdated, it doesn't even begin to cover all the different people we may now count as family. Accordingly, to have a more inclusive policy, it is important to modernize the definition of family, recognize that families come in all shapes and sizes, and allow employees to specify their own "chosen" families.

2. Revise the definition of leave in leave policies: Remember, family-friendly leave policies are family leave policies and not just parental leave policies. Accordingly, those policies should address various times of needs including maternity, paternity, care leave for sick or elderly family members, and time for bereavement. Like modern family setups, it is important to also account for the possible nontraditional setups related to parental leaves.

A good start would be to revise the definition of maternity and paternity to primary and secondary parental leave and give the choice to the couple on the arrangement that suits them best. Following is a definition for each:

- Primary parental leave is provided to the parent who will take the primary responsibility for the care of the new child in their family and would benefit from the longer leave entitlement. This would equally apply in the cases of adoption or surrogacy.
- Secondary parental leave is provided to the parent who is not going to take that primary parental leave but also will be entitled for a leave with a reduced leave entitlement.
- Care leave is provided to employees who need to provide elder care to a member of their chosen family or support in case of serious health condition or long-term illnesses.
- Bereavement time off is time used to account for the death of a member of that chosen family.

Additional to the above, it is worth looking into other options of providing employees with the flexibility to purchase extra days of leave to get additional flexibility in respect of planned time of work. Those will be unpaid with the respective cost being deducted from the employee's salary over their annual leave year. This policy may also contribute to a cost saving from an employer point of view, reduction in absence levels, and an improvement in the level of morale and motivation of people.

3. Help men take parental leave: For the modern generation, fatherhood is being expressed in a totally different way from before. Men are more involved in the upbringing of their kids and want to be present. However, it is still true and unfortunate that most workplaces haven't caught up with this change yet, and dads are still expected to follow the stereotype of putting work as a priority. Accordingly, new dads avoid taking parental leaves for fear of being stigmatized by their employers and missing out on future career opportunities. Therefore, in order to promote inclusion, we need to change the conversation from "women having babies" to "people having babies" and acknowledging the need of fathers to spend more time with their children. Additionally, in order to combat the stigma, it's important to shine a spotlight on male role models across all levels of the business who have taken or plan to take paid paternity, secondary, or primary leave care.

4. Account for all family members in benefit entitlements: Many companies in the Middle East still provide medical insurance only to their employees excluding their families. Additionally, others sometimes offer education assistance to specific senior-

ity levels or support with employees' residencies only excluding families. I understand the financial impact that those extra considerations might lead to and the driver of those decisions, but we cannot ignore the evidence that shows how employers who provide their employees with some family support mechanisms that help them cope with the demands of their non-work lives build loyalty and enhanced commitment. Employees will look for family-friendly employers who are open to working parents and understand their specific needs.

5. Provide onsite support programs for parents, which could come in different forms:

   a. Putting in place mentoring programs specifically designed for working parents to support other parents prior, during, or post their planned primary or secondary parental leaves.

   b. Providing comfortable and hygienic lactation rooms on all sites for mothers to use when they return to work.

   c. Providing schedule flexibility to ensure parents have the time off to attend pre- and post-delivery doctor appointments.

   d. Helping parents of preschool children through onsite childcare or through partnering with childcare centers near the offices.

   e. Arranging for check-in programs to support parents during parental leave to stay in touch with managers and team members to enable a smoother transition back at the end of the leave. This could be a thirty-minute call every week for updates or check-ins.

f.   Planning for family-oriented events like company picnics, parties, and events which include employees' families. Those are highly appreciated by employees and are known to create a stronger sense of belonging within the organization.

Family-friendly workplaces or employers are those whose policies make it possible for employees to easily balance family and work and fulfill both obligations. The trend of promoting family-friendly policies has been recognized in governments as much as global organizations and has been proven to be part of a win-win situation where everyone benefits from the policies. They are good for children, parents, and elders and are in the best interest of the business. Additionally, those are proven to benefit the community and society in general.

It is worth implementing the five strategies that help businesses build inclusive workplaces, but also additional plans that can bring value to people's life. Some might consider, for example, "pawternity" leave given to take care for an ill or injured pet or help integrate a new puppy into their home. Others can consider a form of an extended shared parental leave, or grandparental leave, aimed at compensating working grandparents who give up work or reduce their hours to help with childcare.

Recognizing the benefits of diverse leave options, trends have shown the global upsurge of organizations offering some of the basic paid parental leave to promote family-friendly cultures. Research shows that over the past two years we have seen a significant increase in paid surrogacy leave, paid foster child leave, paid adoption leaves and paid paternity/ maternity leave.

More Organizations Offering Paid Parental Leave

Source: 2018 Employee Benefits (SHRM)

As a commitment to family-friendly cultures, the United Nations celebrated its 2020 International Women's Day with the theme #EachforEqual, intended to spotlight how an equal world would create an enabled world and accordingly challenged organizations to take actions to help forge a gender equal world.

Many organizations have leveraged on this theme to concentrate on the family-friendly policies they have previously revisited and deployed globally to address parental, care, and bereavement paid leaves. Through these policies they have fostered inclusive definitions, embraced all diversities, and promoted inclusive environments that are essential in empowering and meeting the needs of both men and women to manage their unique life and work.

It was so inspiring to get real testimonies from employees who have leveraged those policies and understand how the policies marked their lives. I must mention Michelle who shared publicly how she and her husband recently adopted an eight-year-old boy. Although the situation can be seen as far from traditional, it does not make it any less special for them or in need of different benefits from the traditional parents. It is true that she did not spend her primarily parental leave changing diapers or warming bottles, but she felt as grateful for being able to leverage this leave and spend meaningful time with her child, bonding and sharing experiences that would not have been possible otherwise. Michelle is so thankful for the company that made this happen, and it surely motivated her to give back to this organization.

It is not a secret though that no program or inclusive and family-friendly policy will be as effective in supporting and motivating working parents as much as the role model leaders who balance both the job and the family.

The managers who keep current photos of their children on their desks, visibly leave early sometimes to attend school plays or sports activities, and openly discuss the challenges, energy, and time they put in raising their kids, all the while projecting an upbeat, can-do attitude about work send a powerful message: I can do this so you can, too. Make certain you and everyone in your organization are modeling those behaviors and attitudes you want to see in others.

It has become really apparent that if you want to improve workforce productivity and the company's ability to attract, motivate, and retain employees, you need to invest in family-friendly policies and show your employees you care not only about them, but also about their families and their unique lifestyle.

In this chapter, we have highlighted the need for inclusive terminologies that acknowledge the existing modern family setups, the several policies that can be revisited or introduced to promote inclusiveness, the importance of role models in shedding light on the equal roles of fathers and parenthood, and how family benefits can reinforce employee loyalty. This not only contributes to promoting inclusive work environments but also helps create a world where all are #EachforEqual.

As much as having policies in place is considered important, they must chime with the company's core values. If we speak publicly about the importance of Diversity and Inclusion, gender balance, and equity, we may well want to have family-friendly policies in place, which suit a variety of modern families. Knowing that people's personal and professional lives cannot always be distinctly labeled, offering them the opportunity to fulfill their life goals outside work will make them happier, more fulfilled, and therefore more engaged and productive at work.

While we highlight the topic of gender balance and equity aimed through applying family-friendly policies, it is also imperative to examine the topic of gender pay gaps and pay equity that has taken a lot of the world's attention recently. In the next chapter, we will see how this topic has also been given high priority by many companies that are looking to endorse a gender equal world within their Diversity and Inclusion agendas.

6

EQUAL PAY, EQUAL PAY!

Did you know that the gender pay gap for the FIFA World Cup is $370 million? For those who have not seen the recent news, demands for equal pay in football have been growing louder and louder following the successful staging of the Women's World Cup tournament in France. Apparently for the winning US team, FIFA awarded $30 million to the competing team in the women's tournament, while for last year's Men's World Cup, the total prize money awarded was $400 million, more than ten times as much. This not only fueled strikes and legal actions against FIFA across the globe, but also received a lot of support from the crowd in the stadium, which was chanting, "Equal pay, equal pay!"

FIFA, of course, is not the only culprit when it comes to pay disparity in football or other sports. For that matter, this topic has been recently hitting news headlines across many sectors in the government, in the movie industry, and, of course, in the corporate world. So contrary to widespread belief, the struggle for equal pay did not start in the 1960 with the Equal Pay Act signed in the United States by President John F. Kennedy, but the issue has been taken up by women workers since the late nineteenth century. It is true, however, that now, in the twenty-first century, most people find it obvious that men and women should be paid equal amounts for performing the same job, right? Unfortunately, that is not the case. The gender pay gap is still a significant issue across the globe, and based on United Nations data, still in 2020, women worldwide make only seventy-seven cents for every dollar earned by men, and still women are not receiving equal pay for equal work, let alone equal pay for work of equal value. This not only creates income inequality between men and women, but also hinders the gender balance and equal world we all aim for—an enabled and inclusive world. Therefore, in this chapter we will uncover some of the reasons behind this gender pay gap and actions we can take within our organizations to support closing that gap and drive further inclusion.

Imagine you're a little girl. You're growing up; you go to school; you study as hard as you can with girls, with boys; and you have a dream. You challenge yourself, you work, you sacrifice to get that job you are dreaming of, you work as hard as anyone you know, and then you focus on balancing both your personal and professional responsibilities to continuously grow your career. But then, suddenly, you're told you're not the same as a man, almost as good, but not quite the same . . . Think how devastating and demoralizing that could be and what it would do to you, to your ambitions, and your dreams.

Reality is, women's competencies and skills are still undervalued, and therefore, women frequently still earn less than men for doing comparable jobs—that is, jobs of equal value. As Emma Watson highlighted in the HeforShe UN campaign back in 2014, "If we do nothing, it will take us another seventy-five years before women can expect to be paid the same as men for the same work." Similarly, many economists and professionals have tried to explain the factors behind the wage disparity, which are multifaceted. Research shows that although women have made tremendous strides during the last few decades by moving into jobs and occupations previously done almost exclusively by men, not much has progressed on pay equity in those last two decades. Therefore, this persistent occupation segregation in some industries like the tech, construction, and STEM (science, technology, engineering, maths) roles is still a primary contributor to the lack of significant process in closing the wage gap. Additionally, it is factual to say that having fewer women in senior or more higher-earning roles, or more women working part-time due to their caring responsibilities still play a role in hindering that progress. While the cause for the pay gap can differ between companies, formally communicating and monitoring those pay gaps can help employers identify the reasons for having them in the first place, then help develop action plans to address those gaps.

Closing all gender pay gaps in one go might be a costly exercise for some organizations, and probably an extensive exercise; however, what would be worth considering, instead, is devising a two-to-three-year transitionary plan to address those gaps while accounting for the relevant budget provisions and considerations. It is worth investigating all the situations in which men and women do the same work and where pay gaps are visible, then drawing measurable and realistic plans to adjust pay in accordance to people's years of experiences and relevant performance.

Additionally, there are four supporting actions that can be taken to follow up in closing those gaps:

1. **Implement mentoring programs to upskill women on negotiating their salaries.** Unfortunately, research shows that women are more reluctant and less likely to negotiate their pay. Some even say that a need "to be liked" and the fear of seeming "difficult" keep them from demanding more money. Helping women by offering strategies and tools on the best ways to negotiate and ask for what they believe they are worth will significantly help move the needle on gender pay gap.

After all, it's neither a crime, nor a shame to talk about pay.

2. **Offer transparency in salary structures**. This means being open about processes, policies, and criteria for decision-making when it comes to salary and packages. It also means that employees are clear on what they are entitled to and managers understand that their decisions need to be objective and evidence-based. I have worked for several multinationals that showed with full transparency their pay ranges and reward structures, and I can assure you that it not only helps in reducing pay inequality, but also fortifies trust in leaders and the decision makers.

3. **Apply skill-based assessments when it comes to hiring processes**. Instead of relying only on interviews and personal assessments, ask candidates to showcase and deliver on objective standard tasks they would be expected to perform in the role that they are applying for. Use fair evaluation methods communicated openly to assess their suitability for the role and appoint diversity managers to monitor assessment in this hiring process. The intention is not to assign a police officer within the organization, but rather help reduce biased decisions and encourage accountability.

4. **Stop asking potential hires the question, "What is your current salary?"** I have written about the genderless pay gap on my blog (www.

sarahtabet.com) and how much a similar question can lead to decisions that keep the cycle of income inequality active. People deserve to be paid based on their skills and what they are worth, not be held back by their current or previous salaries. After all, as Letitia James, Attorney General of New York, puts it, "Being underpaid once should not condemn one to a lifetime of inequality."

Even with some of the above measures being recognized globally and applied across many organizations, it is unfortunate that the stubborn inequality in the global average earnings between men and women persists. As per the data published in 2018 by the World Economic Forum, unfortunately, not much progress has been made.

 The Income Gender
Gap 2018

 WORLD
ECONOMIC
FORUM

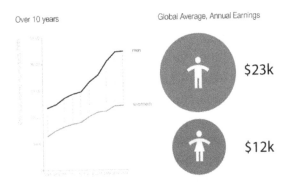

Over 10 years

Global Average, Annual Earnings

men

women

$23k

$12k

Therefore, as mentioned, there is no surprise that gender pay gap has become a widespread topic across industries. Even in Hollywood, Jennifer Lawrence, *The Hunger Games* actress who was the highest paid in the world in 2015 and 2016, revealed for the first time her frustration when she knew she had earned considerably less than her male co-stars in the movie *American Hustle*, despite her major role in the film, and her financial status as a Hollywood A-lister, and being an Oscar winner. She wrote, "I got mad at myself. I failed as a negotiator because I gave up early. I did not want to keep fighting over millions of dollars, and frankly I don't need it. I acknowledge this could be a young person's thing, or it could be a personality thing. I'm sure, for me, it's both, but this is an element of my personality that I've been working against for years, and based on the statistics, I don't think I'm the only woman with this issue." Therefore, to tackle this issue that is prevalent among women, and to address the gender pay gap challenge in general, it is important to recognize that women also have a big responsibility. They need to quit asking themselves questions like, "Are we worth it? Should we have equal pay? Is it socially acceptable that we even talk about pay?" Those questions are sometimes associated with self-esteem, confidence, and self-promotional skills that still need to be sharpened and exercised to be strengthened over time. Women have to be supported to overcome some "modesty norms" and help them facilitate publicly the expression of their self-worth and reject that their skills be undervalued. Instead, what would help is to focus on getting it to the next point of discussing "what is next?"

As covered in this chapter, for us to move the dial on equal pay, we need to debias systems and not only people. As specified, evidence-based design of hiring practices, promotion procedures, and compensation schemes can help organizations do the right and the smart thing to create more inclusive and better workplaces. All these factors are important in evaluating the holistic approach in establishing equal pay processes and impacting the pay structures to help close the gender pay gaps that have been adding up over time.

If we ask ourselves today, almost two hundred years away from the first pay equity movement attempt, where do we really stand when it comes to gender pay equity? The answer would be, we are just not there yet! We all know and truly believe it is time for everyone to acknowledge that there is an issue that is worth fixing. Substantial evidence on the subject argues that pay equity is not only the right thing to do, but it is the smart thing to do for all businesses, and that issue won't change unless both businesses and individuals take intentional actions to fix it. Therefore, in addition to the continuous awareness discussions and actions related to pay equity, it is important to dwell also into the topic of women empowerment and the elements that drive women progression beyond pay. In the next chapter, we'll be looking at the investment opportunities organizations need to create in order to develop women, help them progress, and retain them within the organization.

7

EMPOWERING WOMEN IS
EMPOWERING EVERYONE

Did you know that the World Economic Forum estimates that it will take 257 years to achieve women's economic empowerment and close gender pay gaps in the economy? Even when women empowerment has become a significant topic of discussion in development and economics, still, women's ability to participate equally in existing markets or have access to decent work; have full control over their own time, lives, and bodies; and play a meaningful role in economic decision-making, will only be achieved in 2277, according to the World Economic Forum Global Gender Gap Report.

While the term "economic empowerment" is frequently heard all over the world and actions are seen everywhere, it is shocking to know that at this current pace of change, we will not even live enough to witness the results of the women empowerment we call for or the balance we desire. Yet we cannot deny that women empowerment is a topic that has become more than a women's issue and more of a human matter these days, a prerequisite for a just society as described by the United Nations. Now more than ever, women empowerment is reaching a larger and more globally diverse audience, in part due to the mobilization of women via social media and the support of men globally. Remember Finland's all-female coalition government formed in 2019 and the global celebration and attention it seized? Think also about Natalie Portman's powerful move on the red carpet in 2020 that aimed to honor the female directors who were never nominated for Oscars. Look at the impact of the social media campaigns such as #MeToo and #Timesup. Think about Emirates Airlines among, other aviation companies, who have been proudly advertising the increasing number of women pilots and the programs to recruit more women in the aviation industry. Think about H&M's "She's a Lady" campaign designed to break down gender norms and encourage self-expression of women and the other thousands of global brands supporting women on International Women's Day and sharing their solid actions to grow and develop female pipelines across their organizations. This topic has clearly started leading today's headlines and conversations in governments as much as in the workplace. Women empowerment has become a priority in addressing both the gender gap we have talked about and promoting enhanced Diversity and Inclusion at all levels. However, to get this right, first, everyone must understand how to develop, engage, and retain women, and what does it mean to "empower" them? By the end of this chapter, we will learn more about women empowerment and what actions we can take to embed this into the workplace strategy.

Have you ever wondered why women ask to be empowered? Is it a special power that someone has and is keeping away from women? Even going back into the *Oxford* definition of empowerment, the word itself means "to give someone the authority or power to do something" or "to make someone stronger and more confident." So, who needs to give us power as women, and why do women need permission to be given that power? Coming from a relatively open-minded family and having been treated equally to my male siblings, it just wasn't clear to me. Only recently and within the context of Diversity and Inclusion, I realized the term and understood that it's not actually about women; it is more about the perception of the world around women, as the Australian activist G. D. Anderson rightfully pointed out, "Feminism isn't about making women stronger; women are already strong, it's more about changing the way the world perceives that strength."

For some, women empowerment means tackling the literacy and education aspect, equitable access to health, and ending violence against women, while for others, it is more of a demand for increased participation in decision-making and work and employment, in addition to the involvement in political activities and corporate advancements. The United Nations defines women empowerment as women's sense of self-worth; their right to have and to determine choices; the right to have access to opportunities and resources; and their right to have the power to control their own lives, both within and outside their homes. In order to support that, especially on the corporate level, they have launched the Women's Empowerment Principles, or the WEPs, in 2010 to offer guidance to businesses on how to promote gender equality and empower women within their workplaces. The WEPs is defined by seven principles that companies can adopt and use to draw actions to foster business practices that empower women. It is encouraging to see that today, over two-thirds of companies have a leadership commitment or have demonstrated public support for gender equality and women empowerment, and the list of business leaders who have signed the CEO Statement of Support for the WEPs has grown from thirty-nine in 2010 to over twenty-seven hundred today. This is real proof that companies have been seriously considering and incorporating women empowerment into their corporate strategies, both to ensure sustainable growth and demonstrate leadership through value.

My experience as a woman has taught me that if companies address culture and inclusion as a priority in their business, we would accelerate progress. Not only that, we also have studies which show that women usually reinvest 90% of their income back into their families and communities.

In other words, when we empower women, we empower everyone. If you are a woman yourself or have a daughter, a sister, or a female friend you care about, you have a big responsibility to also contribute to this agenda by creating opportunities for dialogue to influence change. It is important to realize that a big part of the change comes from women themselves. Empowered women empower women!

Unfortunately, some barriers identified in the progression of women relate to their own hesitation to self-promote or to the fact that they do not fully realize their worth and potential to make their substance felt. Therefore, it is important for us as women and men to support women on several aspects:

1. Enhance their self-esteem and self-confidence.
2. Help them see the skills that they possess, that are dormant within them.
3. Develop new skills and capabilities to strengthen them to handle every sphere of their lives.
4. Provide them with the opportunities, facilities, and external and internal environments to utilize their inherent qualities.
5. Ensure equal access to participation and decision-making, be it socially, in the corporate life, or economically.

While encouraging women to lean in and raise their hands higher can help, we must also place equal focus on employers to interfere, act, and fix the problem. There are five main ways to empower women in the workplace and move the needle closer to equality:

1. **Create a culture of mentorship and sponsorship within your organization:** Mentorship relationships can serve as the grain for a close-knit professional network. It offers benefits like access to leadership, advocacy at higher levels, and mutual support. Not only does it help the person being mentored to grow, excel, and advance more effectively, but if done right, it can form the foundation for a valuable professional network that, ultimately, benefits all women within an organization. In parallel, sponsorship at work matters too. It has been said that the biggest decisions about your career are often made when you are not in the room. So, what can you do? It is important to encourage sponsorship to advocate the true work done by women and keep in mind that sponsors, like mentors, can also offer career coaching and guidance that enable others to make more strategic contributions.

2. **Invest in women and in their development and growth.** Investment can be done in several initiatives aimed at women. These can be women networks created in the organization or building and enrolling potential women to leadership programs, exposing women to external conferences

and forums, and, most importantly, investing in training and learning opportunities to equip them with the tools they need to increase their leadership impact and create lasting personal and professional change. It is important to give women the chance to grow and show their capabilities and potential.

3. **Encourage women to make the leap**. Did you know that studies show that men apply for a promotion when they think they meet 60% of the job requirements, while women only apply when they believe they meet 100% of those requirements? This confirms that women need that extra push and encouragement to take more risks and opportunities. So, equal support of partners, mentors, and peers is really ideal for building that self-confidence.

4. **Create more options for women**. This difference between the genders usually occurs when a woman decides to start a family. At this stage, women can decide to play career-focused roles that are less active because of their family obligations, which, obviously, impact their progression in the corporate world. To address that, businesses should create more flexible options for women, including working remotely, part-time, different job opportunities, and consulting—which we have seen in the previous policies—to motivate women and ensure their financial and professional continuity.

5. **Accept and embrace individuality**. Accept that not all women are the same. Yes, I know this seems obvious, but we've all read enough about gender bias to know that there are certain qualities and norms expected of women. Therefore, it is important that you embrace the ways in which women are individuals and don't expect them to adhere to a stereotypical idea of femininity, and don't hold them back when they express their individuality.

It is true that many companies have adopted these and many more actions to support women empowerment in the workplace, targeted either to help women grow or help change the perception of women to the world. Interestingly, some companies have even gone the extra mile by imposing corrective measures on their clients or customers who do not support the same agenda. For example, in a first-of-its-kind global policy, Goldman Sachs Asset Management in February 2020 said that it will vote against dominating committees anywhere in the world that fail to include at least one woman on the board. "We know diversity drives better performance," Koch from Goldman Sachs said. "We've seen it in our business; therefore, we are demanding it of our portfolio companies."

Additionally, Nicole Connolly, head of ESG Investing at Fidelity Investments, told CNBC Make IT that companies in the Russell 3000 Index had to meet one of the following requirements in order to be considered for inclusion in the Women's Leadership Fund:

1. The company has one woman as a member of the senior management team.
2. It is governed by a board that is at least one-third female.
3. It has policies related to parental leave, the gender pay gap, schedule flexibility, etc., all aimed at attracting, retaining, and promoting women.

Similar actions actively show the true determination of companies in helping women to succeed. After all, this is the proof that women empowerment isn't just the most watched show of 2020; it is a top priority for leaders. Therefore, their job is to demonstrate how this is a business priority by what they say, what they do, what they measure, and how they lead.

If I reflect on my own personal journey as a woman working in a company that is truly committed to developing and empowering women, I cannot but mention the endless benefits of being part of women networks, being nominated for and partaking in women leadership programs, being connected to supportive mentors and coaches, and backed by sponsors and amazing managers who played a pivotal role in progressing my career. Given these opportunities, I was able to build wider networks and meet like-minded individuals and great leaders who are as passionate about the D&I topic and helped me speak louder about the importance of inclusive cultures and mindsets and helped drive the same agenda within their workplaces. I have encountered amazing role models, men and women, who have also helped me understand my strengths and improvement areas to advance both as a leader and as an individual. In women forums and mentoring programs, I had fruitful conversations with women leaders, mentors, and coaches and learned how some have successfully managed their personal and professional life requirements and achieved work-life harmony. I can share endless examples of how the investment made in my development as a woman and as a leader, in addition to my personal ambition to thrive, has helped me lean in and feel truly empowered and empower others in return.

Needless to mention how more awareness and conversation on women empowerment can be truly a good thing, but sometimes I cannot but wonder, is this "noise" masking a lack of real action and progress? It is unfortunate that, despite progress, still in S&P 500 companies, the higher up the corporate ladder, the fewer the women. Very few women are CEOs of the world's largest corporations, and still in the May 2019 *Fortune* list, only thirty-three women (6.6%) were CEOs of *Fortune* 500 companies. So, what more can be done to influence those numbers?

To see improvement, we need to remember first that women make up half of the world's talent pool; thus, including them is not an option, not a luxury, it is a mandate. The most powerful thing we can do as organizations is to create a culture of "conscious inclusion." This is not only about building the desire, vision, and capacity of people to make decisions, but it is also about leading, thinking, and acting with the conscious intent of including everyone.

Empowering women has been proven to be crucial in creating inclusive and open workplaces, which in turn benefits the business. To support that agenda, individually or on the corporate level, it is key to understand what is truly required for women to be empowered, stay, and strive to climb the corporate ladder. As seen in this chapter, there could be many internal and external factors that can be holding women back, but what remains important is to be explicit about progressing women and helping them obtain the skills and experience to manage and drive the business in both operational and the strategic positions.

This decade is a moment for companies to prove they can turn their commitments into action. It is worth digging deeper and understanding the reasons hindering women empowerment. Is it lack of confidence, discomfort in self-promotion, or absence of self-assertion? Will investment in their development, proper nurturing, and polishing and sharpening of their skills help them become stronger? Will exposing them through mentors and sponsors or providing flexible arrangements improve their engagement and willingness to stay and guarantee their success? Start by asking yourself what small and big actions you can do to invest in that purpose and make sure to hit the accelerator in building an equal and inclusive future. Not only women depend on it, but also our economic growth, workforce participation, and future generations.

Finally, when we think of struggles for empowerment, inclusion, and equality, we think of heroes who have fought for women's rights—luminary individuals like Malala Yousafzai (Pakistani teenager activist advocating for female education and the youngest Nobel laureate) and other female leaders who have changed the game for women at work, like Sheryl Sandberg (COO of Facebook). They have inspired others to shape feminism, brought equality to society, and demonstrated true inclusive leadership. In the next chapter, we will be looking to understand the term "inclusive leadership" and how our behaviors can impact our decisions and judgments and might hinder or accelerate the progress of inclusion.

8

ARE YOU AN INCLUSIVE LEADER?

Thais Compoint, author of *Succeed As an Inclusive Leader*, says, "Inclusive leadership is not a destination, it is a journey that requires humility, curiosity, and courage."

It is no secret that in today's world, the cost of bad leadership behavior is mounting for shareholders and across organizations. Many CEOs and high-profile leaders have been expelled on the allegations of discrimination, harassment, and other offenses or signs of exclusion that might once have been swept under the rug. One of the factors accounted for while assessing those leadership behaviors is inclusive leadership, and how much leaders pay attention to that dimension.

Inclusive leadership is not a new idea; the concept was introduced more than three decades ago. However, back then there was no good way to assess inclusion, let alone track a leader's progress toward inclusiveness. Many employers were, and still are, focusing on attracting diverse groups of employees, increasing representation of women or minorities, investing in development, or creating policies and procedures to support inclusion without paying much attention to the mindsets of leaders that is essential in making their organizations inclusive. In this chapter, we will learn more about inclusive leadership and the sorts of behaviors that have become the hallmarks of inclusive leaders. Additionally, you, as leader, will also be able to measure your inclusiveness and realize your development opportunities.

Have you ever worked for an inclusive leader? If you have, you would know it. These leaders are special because of the positive impact they create on individuals and organizations. They are leaders who actively seek and consider other perspectives to take decisions. They see diversity as a competitive edge and understand the value of having everyone's voice heard. They encourage and develop the best in others and spotlight their achievements. While if you've worked for a non-inclusive leader, you may have thought about leaving more than staying.

Not too long ago, leaders were basically defined as people who had all the answers. They had to figure out what to do and then tell people when, where, and how to do it. Today's managers and leaders, however, face a whole new set of expectations in the way they motivate others who work with them. Even organizations are different. They are flatter, more collaborative, and more diverse. Therefore, for leaders to succeed, they need to recognize that the commanding style isn't most effective anymore, and rather than taking a top-down approach, they must ask for other people's opinion and insights, display the ability to embrace individual differences, amplify the strength of diverse people, and potentially leverage them for competitive advantage. This is what defines inclusive leadership. It refers to the mindsets, knowledge, skills, and behaviors that leaders possess, and the competencies they need to develop.

People say that they truly want to be inclusive leaders, but what would that be like? The first step in understanding more about what it takes to be inclusive and how to get there is taking a quick self-test intended to highlight what strengths and areas of opportunity one has as a leader. How about you? Are you an inclusive leader? Are you willing to know more? If so, let's get started by answering the below eight questions.

1. Do I know my personal strengths and weaknesses?
2. Am I self-aware of how preconceived views can influence my behaviors toward others?
3. Do I treat others with respect and value everybody's worth without judgment?
4. Do I listen before talking, observe, and learn from others?

5. Do I openly admit I made a mistake?
6. Do I concentrate on the skills and strengths of others, paying less attention to their deficits and weaknesses?
7. Am I able to create a positive and safe working environment that offers opportunities for everyone to display innovation and creativity?
8. Do I invite people to speak up and give their views and opinions even if those might be opposing to mine?

Reflecting on these questions would help you measure your own behavioral competencies and identify areas where greater inclusivity is needed and where you need to cultivate skills to act in a more inclusive way. To become a better inclusive leader and train others, it is worth reflecting on the self-test and additionally consider the following eight steps toward inclusion:

1. Encourage everyone to build a diverse network; include and seek inputs from people across a wide variety of backgrounds.
2. Check your assumptions about people, cultivate a nonjudgmental attitude toward differences, and ask, "Are my assumptions based on facts?"
3. Participate in meetings and discussions with a positive and open mind. Engage in constructive conversation, address misunderstandings, resolve

disagreements, act to reduce stressful situations, and ensure you prevent any exclusions. Don't overlook the "small" stuff, and when you witness someone being rude or dismissive, call it out.

4. Slow your response, listen carefully to the person speaking until they feel understood, and make a habit of asking questions to ensure your response is relevant.

5. Scan social dynamics and interaction patterns. Are some team members more dominant and others more passive and quieter? Make sure to involve those passive participants and give everyone a voice.

6. Deepen self-awareness and awareness of others. Ask, "What is it like to be on the other side of me?"

7. Use inclusive language. If you think about it, most of our communication involves gendered language and commonly include words that assume connections between jobs or role and gender, like policeman, for example. Be more mindful of the language you use, and make sure it's as inclusive as possible. Some interesting examples published by the UN women are listed below.

If you don't know someone's gender or when talking about a group, use gender-neutral language.

~~mankind~~	humankind
~~chairman~~	chair
~~congressman~~	legislator
~~businessman~~	representative
~~policeman~~	police officer
~~landlord~~	owner
~~boyfriend/girlfriend~~	partner
~~salesman~~	salesperson
~~manpower~~	workforce
~~maiden name~~	family name
~~fireman~~	firefighter
~~husband/wife~~	spouse

UN WOMEN

8. Engage and motivate others in learning about differences and experiences nonjudgmentally. Speak with others about the importance of cultural agility, which is the ability to listen, communicate, understand, and respond authentically across boundaries of differences.

By focusing on these tips and tricks to become a more inclusive leader, you will also be able to promote inclusiveness in society and the workplace. Inclusive leadership seems to have become a popular topic in the last few years, and many models have been created to identify the traits of inclusive leaders, in addition to the several assessments showcasing the new leadership dimensions. A popular one is the Everything DiSC® online personality test, which is one of the most significantly validated tools available. It showcases eight individual leadership styles and clarifies why they are important.

The eight dimensions of leadership have been categorized as, "Pioneering, Energizing, Affirming, Inclusive, Humble, Deliberate, Resolute, and Commanding." Each will provide aspects of strength and areas of development to help increase flexibility in leadership behaviors.

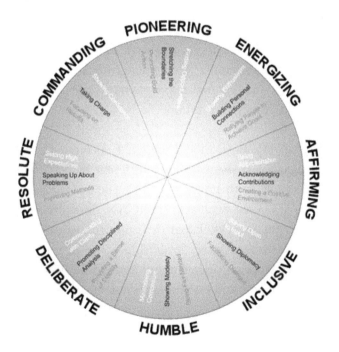

Therefore, referring to DISC and specifically to what "Inclusive" means in this context, it assesses leaders based on how open they are to other people's input, how diplomatic they are in their style, and how much they can facilitate dialogue among a diverse group of people. Other inclusion experts like Hayley Barnard and Thais Compoint also define inclusive leaders, respectively, as being FAST (fair, taking action, self-aware and building trust) or describe their journey to inclusive leadership as one that requires humility, curiosity, and courage.

All in all, what is clear is that inclusion has strongly become one of the essential expectations of today's leadership behaviors, and being a "good enough" leader doesn't even come close to what makes people motivated and engaged in a team or an organization.

Being an HR professional myself, I encounter hundreds of leaders every day who have different leadership styles. Interestingly, with my access to the many available tools like LVI (360) feedback, HOGAN assessments, and engagement surveys, I had the opportunity to firsthand track and link inclusive leadership styles to the positive employee work engagement and how both effective organizational commitment and employee creativity mediated this relationship.

Inclusive leaders are seen as the driving force behind their employees. They know how to encourage people to contribute their best in their roles to respond to the organization's needs. All the relevant leadership assessment tools have proven how much employees want to work with leaders who show openness, availability, and accessibility in their interactions within their teams, and how they want to be led through participation. Employees want to contribute to every aspect of the job and to every decision and want to feel their contribution is accounted for, regardless of how unconventional their input might be. They not only do not want to be told what to do by leaders and managers anymore, in most cases, they simply won't accept it. Fundamentally, today's workforce will only accept to work with inclusive leaders, the kind of leaders who are seen to cast a long shadow. So, if you want to lead inclusively, you need to consciously commit to developing the skills necessary for today's "guide and inspire" environment and model those inclusive behaviors within a two-way trusting relationship with people. Because they are a set of behaviors and not personal epiphanies (Aha moments you might get), you need to work hard on building them through coaching and practice which would quickly create observable impact on you and on others. Like the age-old question about leadership, are some people naturally more inclusive, or is inclusive leadership nurtured over time?

It seems that people who are naturally curious about others—about their cultures and experiences—tend to be more inclusive. But anyone can learn to be more inclusive by practicing these key behaviors shared earlier and discussed in this chapter. As a next step, start by self-assessing against common inclusive behaviors, and ask yourself, "How do I define inclusion in the context of my environment? Can I recall a particular experience where I felt included? Based on that, can I describe what inclusion feels like for me?" Asking these questions will help you become more self-aware and will help support your agenda in becoming a true inclusive leader.

Marking that, it is also important to realize that inclusive leaders have biases and blind spots. They are aware of conscious and unconscious biases that are built in and are very much so realistic. In the next chapter, we will understand more about those biases and how they influence our behaviors to help us act toward inclusion.

9

THINK YOU ARE NOT BIASED?
THINK AGAIN

"Think of driving your car down the highway. You want to shift into the right lane, so you click your turn signal and look into your rear and side-view mirrors. It's all clear. You start to make your way over to the next lane, and then a car horn blasts and you swerve back into your lane, realizing you just missed crashing into a car that was in that right lane you didn't see because it was in your car's blind spot. Just like that car, we too sometimes don't see what's in another lane. Unconscious bias is a blind spot that can cause damage because you don't know it's there" (Susan Taylor, CEO of Generon International).

As human beings, we naturally perceive people and make judgments quickly. This is not an evolutionary error, but it is rather due to unconscious shortcuts that our brain makes to be able to quickly sort, categorize, and make calls based on limited pieces of information we might have. The unconscious processing abilities of the human brain are estimated at roughly eleven million pieces of information per second in comparison to our conscious processing, which is estimated to reach forty pieces per second. Therefore, it is no secret that creating those mental shortcuts can help us keep up with all of the stimuli around us. Knowing that they happen naturally, taking shortcuts to make decisions can impact the quality of our decision-making and can make our decisions unfair toward others. These unconscious shortcuts are also referred to as hidden biases that may be conscious or unconscious and might have positive or negative consequences.

In this chapter, we will learn how to realize these biases, understand more about the possible consequences, and, most importantly, focus on how to behave more inclusively in order to mitigate some of these biases.

Despite adopting some of the actions we have covered earlier to improve and promote inclusion in the workplace or in society, plus the efforts we might have set out to create and nurture a culture of inclusion, there are still some subtle ways in which our unconscious thoughts would betray these efforts. Although most people like to think that they are fully in control of their feelings and the way they act toward others, research suggests otherwise. Considerable evidence now supports that we are all susceptible to bias that is not only limited to ethnicity and race, as many might think, but may exist toward any group based on one's age, gender, physical abilities, religion, sexual orientation, weight, and many other characteristics.

We have a bias when we have a preference for someone or something or an attitude toward them with or without our conscious knowledge. A common example of this is seen in studies that show that white people will frequently associate criminality with black people without even realizing they are doing it. Think about COVID-19. How many have initially and unconsciously freaked out while walking on the streets and bumping into Asians? How many have avoided any kind of interaction with Asians for the fear of infection? Well, COVID-19 pandemic, like various other pandemics, tends to provoke xenophobia and bias. An increasing number of news channels have reported instances of bias, harassment, and bullying directed at people perceived to be of Asian descent following the spread of the new coronavirus. Although this is a clear example of bias related to race, it's also important to clarify that research identifies more than a hundred biases that affect how we make decisions every day.

Due to the numerous types of biases, it is very challenging, of course, to cover them all. Instead, we will focus on those that cause the most unfairness as described by psychologists. The five most common biases are defined as confirmation bias, self-serving bias, affinity bias, bandwagon effect, and stereotyping.

1. Confirmation bias is when we look to prove our own point of view and ignore any information that might contradict that. When we speak to others, we commonly favor ideas that confirm our existing beliefs and try to find resources that justify what we believe in. This is very typical during an election season, for example, when people tend to seek positive information that paints their favorite candidates positively and seek only negative information related to the opposing candidates.

2. Self-serving bias is when we feature our successes to our doing, lying in our own glory when things go right, but when we face failure, we tend to attribute these events to other people or external factors. This could sometimes mean evading personal responsibility for our actions as a defense mechanism to protect our self-esteem. A simple example of that is during performance evaluations when we sometimes blame others for our own failures.

3. Affinity bias is when we favor people that are like us over others who are different from us. This can happen in hiring; promoting; and in our general tendency to get along, socialize, and spend time with others who have the same hobbies as us, have been to the same schools, come from the same country, or share other common attributes. This is also linked to the love of similarity that we've talked earlier about.

4. Bandwagon effect is when we do things primarily because others are doing it. We ignore our views and perspectives and adopt others'. This happens in many cases when others are either more senior to us or more influential than us. Interestingly, research has shown that 75% of people might give answers that they know are false simply because others around them gave that incorrect answer.

5. Stereotyping is when we categorize and label people who share a particular characteristic. This is common in biases based on gender, race, ethnicity, and physical features. COVID-19 impact on Asians is a good example of this bias.

After understanding the types of biases, we have to know that confronting them requires a careful approach because most people are not aware of them. We should be aware though that unconscious biases are not permanent. In fact, they are malleable, and there are some steps we can take, especially in the workplace, to limit their impact on our thoughts and behaviors:

1. As with any far-reaching initiative, it is important that everyone knows it is a priority. It is critical to raise awareness and openly share that you are making bias mitigation a priority with a company-wide announcement.

2. It is important to facilitate discussions and training sessions across the organization and encourage an

open dialogue where people can share examples of some biases they often notice and are exposed to.

3. Make sure that the decision-making process uses objective criteria and make sure to clarify to everyone how the decisions will be made. If people keep their implicit biases in mind when evaluating performance, or maybe hire or nominate people for promotion, they are less likely to lean on mental shortcuts. Nowadays, the increased use of artificial intelligence and recruitment robots in the hiring process, for example, has proven successful in mitigating biases.

4. Practice inclusive behavior. Put yourself in other people's shoes; be proactively curious. Involve everyone in discussions, monitor and take their responses by affirming them, highlight the areas of agreement, and isolate the points of differences.

5. Do not be a bystander. Bystanders are those who see or become aware of biases but do nothing about it. Make sure you step in to provide support to victims of bias; hold decision-makers accountable, including yourself; and make sure to call out for exclusions.

Individual strategies like these, in addition to the serious measures taken to create social awareness, will help everyone address unconscious bias. A great example of an effective measure taken recently by the WHO to mitigate and combat the upsurge in stereotyping bias as a result of COVID-19 is strongly recommending against linking communicable diseases to specific geographic regions. For example, referring to COVID-19 as the China virus or the Wuhan virus and asking that all governments refrain from that use. This act, by itself has proven to reduce the bias seen and felt toward Asians all around the globe.

Knowing that our unconscious train of thought cannot sometimes be controlled, we can always accept that these beliefs are not our fault. It does not make us bad people and surely does not make us explicitly racist. However, it is critical to assume that a society motivated by uncontrolled unconscious beliefs is dangerous for everyone and can lead to an extreme social backlash.

Luckily, studies show that being self-aware reduces the extent to which some biases come into play in our lives. Simply reading about biases and being more self-aware of our feelings and beliefs can help us move toward an honest social progress. To help us do that, we can recognize our own biases using the implicit association tests (or other instruments to assess bias). These tests are very popular in studying biases and are a validated tool to measure implicit behaviors that we might not be aware of. Implicit association tests can be found online, and most are free of charge.

In parallel, as part of my own efforts in creating awareness on unconscious bias and highlighting the importance of self-awareness within my team and the organization, I have run a small challenge in a recent leadership team meeting to help the team examine their own possible biases and understand the roots of stereotype. The challenge was in a form of a riddle:

A father and his son were in a car crash and were rushed to the hospital. The father died. The boy is taken to the operating room and the doctor says, "I cannot operate on this boy because he is my son."

How is this possible?

In this forum, unfortunately, only one out of the twelve senior people present in the room was able to accurately figure it out. This was additional proof for me and for others that we still need to consistently make efforts across all the levels of the organization to talk about unconscious bias and stress on the possible mitigation plan. For the fun of it, I will not give you the answer to this test in my book and will leave it open to you to address and hopefully figure it out (without Googling it, of course☺).

Regardless of the plans we make on an individual level or organizational level to address biases, the key to success for all these plans will always be full-scale commitment. Piecemeal or ad hoc initiatives cannot do the job. Mitigating of biases must begin with every individual understanding the importance and impact of hidden biases in our day-to-day decision-making and have the support from top management cascaded throughout every aspect of the organization to eventually impact both change in mindset and language.

Knowing that emphasizing on the topic of biases is important in committing to Diversity and Inclusion and the way we interact with others, we have captured in this chapter the common types of biases we see in our workplaces or in society and some techniques we can use to make our judgments more balanced.

We all like to think we are open-minded and nonjudgmental. In fact, each one of us tends to believe he or she is fairer and holds less bias than the average person. However, unconscious bias is something that affects us all, and the question we should ask ourselves is not, do we have a bias? But rather, what are our biases? Let us admit that we are not very familiar with the cultures, values, and practices of people whose backgrounds are not the same as ours, and let's be willing to take that extra step of reconfirming whether we are basing our decisions on thirty-second judgments or on quantitative and qualitative information. Once we become more conscious about this, our decisions will become fairer and more informed, and our behaviors will become more just.

Being inclusive is a journey often mistaken for a destination. On this journey, we learn many lessons: how to promote Diversity and Inclusion in our workplace, what

policies and practices can support that, the basics of inclusive leadership, and the unconscious biases that impact our
judgment and our view of the world. Additionally, we must
also be willing to explore not only how our minds work
unconsciously, but also how even small insensitive actions
or remarks, defined as microaggressions, can impact other
people's lives and promote exclusion. In the next chapter, we will examine microaggressions, which are closely
tied to hidden biases, and how they can further sponsor
stereotyping.

10

BUT YOU ALL LOOK ALIKE

When you speak, all of you speaks.

—*Therapist Virginia Satir*

Have you heard of the term, "Death by a thousand cuts?" Aside from Taylor Swift's song, this term was used in an article published in 2013 by the journal of LGBT youth to describe microaggressions and their impact on people. If we believe that one discriminatory experience is horrible, how can we measure the several experiences that could be happening over the course of an entire lifetime? For many, this impact can be deadly by even more than a thousand cuts.

You have done it and it's been done unto you. You shake a person's hand but rarely make eye contact. You attend a colleague's presentation and repeatedly glance down at your phone. You "listen" while peeking at a WhatsApp message . . . It turns out that these seemingly unrelated acts of disrespect have a name; they are called microaggressions. They are a subset of the estimated two thousand to four thousand micro-messages that individuals send every day to one another. Although thought to be harmless, they have been proven to demoralize people. Some have impacts that go far deeper than what meets the eye. They are rooted in powerful biases that are often subconscious. In this chapter we will learn more about micro-messages and microaggressions. What are they, and how we can avoid them to promote inclusion?

A big part of our communication happens through micro-messages. These are subtle everyday communications which come through what we say and how we behave and are often delivered subconsciously. They can positively contribute to inclusion or negatively detract from it. Think for a moment: Have you ever been asked for your input into a discussion? Have been publicly praised for your hard work? Have been in a meeting where your name was remembered by someone you met once years ago? How did it feel?

These acts, although they might seem trivial, are gestures of inclusion and are an acknowledgment of a person's values. They are referred to as micro-affirmations and basically mean being nice humans to everyone.

In contrast, think again: Have you been ever called the wrong name in a meeting? Have your contributions to a discussion in a meeting been ignored? Have you been in a situation where you knew that someone was hearing you but not "listening" to you? In psychology, these small exclusions are referred to as microaggressions.

However you slice it, these mini-messages have a cumulative effect on the morale and productivity of a person. How could they not? They send a fundamental message about how a person is appreciated, valued, thought of, and is regarded. Together micro-affirmations and microaggressions are called micro-messages. However subtle, they can make or break the sense of inclusion.

Although these are small examples of microaggressions that might or might not have happened to you, I challenge you to plead unguilty for never realizing any of the following:

1. Sighed loudly in a meeting.
2. Interrupted a person mid-sentence.
3. Dismissed someone's contribution.
4. Rolled your eyes during a meeting.
5. Checked your e-mail or phone during a face-to-face meeting
6. Deliberately excluded someone in an e-mail.

If you have, then you have unconsciously displayed a micro-aggression which can contain a hidden insult to someone. And a key part of what makes microaggressions so disconcerting is that they happen casually, frequently, and often without any harm intended, in everyday life. Although some might think microaggressions simply describe situations in which people are being much too sensitive or naive, they have actually been proven to lower confidence of people, reduce their engagement, hinder performance, impact mental health, and make people feel small. So, what can we do to avoid them?

We've all heard the saying, "The devil is in the details." And this is true in combating microaggressions. To avoid them and better manage them, we need to create magic. M-A-G-I-C.

Make eye contact, smile, and use people's name when conversing with them.

Acknowledge the small things people do and share their accomplishments publicly.

Give your complete attention to people when they are speaking. Be present, and let your body language and facial expression demonstrate that you are listening.

Invite others to share their views and input at every opportunity.

Create awareness, and make sure to give specific and sincere feedback to people when they display microaggressions. Focus on the event and not on the person as the goal is not to make others feel bad but is more about helping them understand how their comments or actions can be hurtful.

Chester M. Pierce, the Harvard psychiatrist, created the term "microaggressions" in 1970. Originally the term was linked to race and applied to the insults and dismisses geared toward black people from white Americans. In 1973, Mary Rowe, an MIT economist, extended the meaning of microaggressions to include aggressions against women. Today, however, the definition includes discriminatory comments made toward everyone and linked to gender, race, ethnicity, sexual orientation, age, disability, religious affiliations, and much more. A comment like "But you all look alike" is linked to race. "She is 50. She might not be a right fit for the job," refers to age. "Wow, I'm surprised you're a woman and good at math," refers to gender. "You're being paranoid," refers to mental health. "Wow, I'm so surprised you don't look or sound gay," refers to sexual orientation. And, "Ugh, I can't read, I'm totally dyslexic today," refers to disability.

All those are examples of microaggressions that still happen every day and are thought of implicit biases come to life in our everyday interactions. Acknowledging this, it is not surprising that over the past few years several campaigns have shined the light on microaggressions and have highlighted commonly used ones to create awareness.

In the United States since 2014, and in order to address racism, bias, and discrimination on campuses, students have organized "I too am Harvard" campaign primarily to illustrate the personal experiences of black students at Harvard University. Inspired by that, minority students at McGill University, the University of Oxford, and the University of Cambridge have also developed similar multimedia campaigns to address biases and strengthen a sense of belonging among all community members. Additionally, workshops have been offered to provide all participants basic knowledge about bias and microaggressions along with the tools to identify and respond to them. This topic is not only a nationwide focus but has also become a globally recognized one. Even Sheryl Sandberg, in the corporate context, nicely addresses gender microaggressions she faces due to her role as a woman and a leader by clearly stating, "In the future there will be no female leaders. There will be just leaders."

Unfortunately, even with the rise in awareness, we still see a spike in hate crimes across the globe like the recent #Blacklivesmatter campaign and anti-racism protests and many others that are bias motivated and result from the accumulated impact of certain microaggressions delivered incessantly. Therefore, to see true positive results in combating them, it is important that we highlight ways to respond and cope when confronted with microaggressive acts.

As a start, it is critical for us to be reasonable, not overreact, pause, and ask ourselves a series of questions. Did this microaggression really occur? Was it deliberate or unintentional? Should I respond to this microaggression? And if so, how should I respond?

A good starting point would be to assume that there is no malicious intent, approach the situation with a positive attitude, give the individual the benefit of the doubt, discuss your feelings about the impact of the incidents, try to understand the situation, and be empathetic. Remember, as most microaggressions are unconscious, probability is that we have all done or said something that unintentionally offended someone.

In this chapter we have learned about micro-messages and shared examples of both micro-affirmations and microaggressions, which although seemingly small and sometimes innocent can take a real psychological toll on the mental health of their recipients. If negative, this toll can lead to anger and crime on the social level and can lower work productivity and problem-solving abilities in a workplace environment.

Learning about them and some of the strategies that help us combat them, we recognize that it's not very hard to put some thought into the biases we might hold and microaggressions we might commit. We live in a time where it is crucial that we become more conscious about the ways our words and actions are perceived by others. We need to listen when people explain why certain remarks offend them and make it a habit to stop for a beat and think before we speak.

We all have responsibility to our community and in our workplaces to foster healthy, inclusive environments. Knowing that we are all subject to microaggressions that are mostly unintentional, let's play our role in identifying them, recognize the impact they have on us and on others, and begin to create MAGIC to help shift our culture.

In the next chapter, we will look into the importance of mindset to culture and tackle Inclusion in the social context.

11

AN INCLUSIVE SOCIETY IS A SOCIETY FOR ALL!

Jesse Jackson says, "When everyone is included, everyone wins."

Back in 1995, the first World Summit for Social Development was held in Copenhagen, calling in governments from all around the world to discuss how they can put people at the center of their development plans. In this conference of world leaders, the largest ever at that time, the term "inclusive society" was defined for the first time. It has been described as "Society for all in which every individual, each with rights and responsibilities has an active role to play." It is a society aimed to account for human rights, cultural and religious diversities, social justice, and the special needs of vulnerable and disadvantaged groups. Since then, we have seen governments, through their public sector initiatives, fostering social integration, and endorsing inclusion in their social development agendas. However, a lot has also materialized in the private sector, where the value of inclusion has equally been reinforced.

In the past few chapters we have touched on ways to promote inclusion in the workplace and the impact of that on society and communities; there have also been a lot of parallel social developments and transformations across several sectors that have been equally important in embracing an inclusive and enabled world. In this chapter, we will be touching upon some of the inspiring stories that influenced transformations and the factors key to their success.

Have you heard of inclusive fashion? A term that has come into vogue lately not only to advertise how the most prominent fashion weeks have started including differently abled models on runaways or how models of different ethnicities can be found on catwalks and billboards around the world, but also to spotlight how inclusion has become more of a norm, not only a buzzword in the fashion industry.

Fashion has taken measures to become more inclusive in many ways. In 2019, *Vogue Arabia* enlisted not one, but two voluptuous models on its front cover with its #beautybeyondsize. Brands like Tommy Hilfiger and Christiano Krosh have started designing with wheelchair users in mind, and fashion media has been giving more and more attention to different types of beauty. Additionally, and more importantly, the mindset of design has shifted to blend both fashion and function to create what is called "adaptive clothing." An excellent example of adaptive clothing is "Myself Belts" created by the ingenious Talia Goldfarb, featuring belts that can be fastened and unfastened with one hand. That idea, as simple as it is, has proven to be extremely effective for kids with autism, Down syndrome, delay in fine motor skills, and other medical conditions, and it has been highlighted as a great idea for promoting independence of children.

Truth be told, I personally had never given much thought to some of the struggles differently abled people have when it comes to clothing, but I'm fascinated by some of the fashion companies that made it their prime concern to change fashion in a way that meets the diverse needs of society. These changes have been detected not only in fashion but also in the toys industry. For example, Barbie, the classic children's doll, kicked off the new decade with a renewed push for more diverse and inclusive offerings to champion the topic of Diversity and Inclusion among children and their parents. The 2020 collection has been released to show off a multidimensional view of beauty and fashion. One doll was released with vitiligo, a condition that causes the loss of skin pigments and blotches, aimed to raise global awareness on this condition. Other dolls have also been introduced without hair, with wheelchairs, with darker skin tone, and a gold prosthetic limb. Although Barbie has been often criticized for promoting one kind of unrealistic body image, it has made it a point to change a lot over the years, answering pleas for the iconic doll to be made more inclusive.

The need for extended inclusion is everywhere, and the progress seen in some major industries is truly encouraging. Well, guess what? It's also replicable. As Theodore Melfi, the American screenwriter, film director, and producer, puts it, "You all have the responsibility to make inclusion a daily thought so we can get rid of the word inclusion." It is true that you and everyone else can create an impact and promote inclusion wherever you are and whatever you do. All it takes is an open mind and a growth mindset.

Talking about growth mindset and thanks to the work of Carol Dweck, PhD and Professor of Psychology at Stanford University, many people have become familiar with the term "growth mindset" and the impact of mindset on behavior. Doctor Dweck studies human motivation and has spent extensive time diving into why people succeed (or not) and what's within our control to cultivate success.

In her research and published work, she describes two main mindsets we can navigate life with—growth and fixed. Much of what we think we understand of our personality comes from our mindsets. This both pushes us and prevents us from filling our potential. People in a fixed mindset believe they are either good or aren't good at something based on their intrinsic nature because it's just who they are. In a fixed mindset, usually we stick with what we know to keep our confidence. We look inside ourselves for our true passion and purpose as if this is a hidden inherent thing. Failures define us, and we feel we are either naturally great or will never be great. In a growth mindset, however, we believe anyone can be good at anything; skill comes with practice, and abilities are entirely due to us and our actions.

As Doctor Dweck explains in her studies, however, nobody is all one or the other. "Everyone is actually a mixture of fixed and growth mindsets, and that mixture continuously evolves with experience." As we begin to understand the fixed and growth mindsets, we will see exactly how all our ideas about risk taking and effort comes from that mindset. It helps us realize the value of challenging ourselves and putting in efforts to learn and grow.

To dwell deeper into the fixed and growth mindset I have added some snapshots of the characteristics of each as described by Doctor Dweck in her book, *Mindset: The New Psychology of Success*. She explains how changing even the simplest of our beliefs can have a profound impact on nearly every aspect of our lives. It is worth mentioning that her work has become equally popular in the corporate world, and I personally have used much of her research as training material to stimulate a high-performance culture across the organization.

Characteristics of a Fixed Mindset	Characteristics of a Growth Mindset
• Believes intelligence and talent are fixed	• Believes intelligence and talents can be developed
• Believes effort is fruitless	• Believes effort is the path to mastery
• Believes failures define who they are	• Believes mistakes are part of learning
• Hides flaws	• Views failure as an opportunity
• Avoids challenges	• Believes failures are temporary
• Ignores feedback	• Embraces challenges
• Views feedback as personal criticism	• Welcomes feedback
• Feels threatened by other's success	• Views other's success as inspirational

A great example of someone who has displayed a growth mindset was Talia Goldfarb with "Myself Belts" who took a bold risk and challenged existing conditions to improve the position of some excluded members of the community. With her efforts, she was able to upgrade a basic accessory that has existed since the 1930s to enact a possible social imprint.

Also, who would ever think that sharing one photo on Instagram would inspire legislators to create new laws? This relates to another story of an amazing person who demonstrated a growth mindset, challenged the status quo, and personally led a transformation. This person is Donte Palmer. Two years ago, Donte Palmer, a father of three boys living in Florida, started the #SquatForChange movement on his Instagram account, aiming to show how dads must change their children's nappies on their laps as there are no changing tables in men's bathrooms.

Not knowing he was about to start a global movement, he posted an Instagram picture showing how he is being forced to squat down in the toilets to change his baby's nappies, and he typed, "This is serious a post!!! What's the deal with not having changing tables in men's bathrooms as if we don't exist? #FLM# Fatherslivesmatter. Clearly, we do this often because look how comfortable my son is. It's routine to him!!!Let's fix this problem!"

Overnight that post went viral. Men from all over the world started submitting pictures of themselves squatting too while changing for their kids, and parents from every corner of the globe reached out for support and reinforcement of the movement.

Now, after two years of campaigning, a law came into effect. As of January 2020, all new or renovated buildings in New York with public bathrooms are required to make changing tables available to both men and women. Donte shared with the news, "I am truly excited and honored to be an individual/father that is changing the world by sharing the frustrations of parents everywhere. It's amazing how one nonpartisan issue can bring a lot of people together as parents, regardless of backgrounds, culture, and sexual orientation. #SquatForChange is not just a movement, but a lifestyle, and it shows that with hard work and dedication, one person can change the world." Indeed Donte, with his mindset and dedication, has literally changed the world to become a more equal and inclusive world.

Despite the favorable global evolution we witness around inclusion, we still sometimes feel that there is a great deal to go when we see groups in the news and social media pit themselves against each other with so much mistrust and anger. Bias is still there, and discrimination and hate crimes still happen. So, what more can we do?

I believe that in order to anticipate uninterrupted positive development, we need constructive interruption. Constructive interruption is when we pause, reflect, think creatively, and are willing to dare to disrupt our traditional beliefs and ways of operations. Since we are not naturally inclined to interrupt ourselves, we need to ensure that this happens in the right place and the right time.

For constructive introduction to work and in order to create truly inclusive communities, we must impact, as a priority, the youngest members of our society: children. Inclusion is about learning to live with one another, including those with special needs and limitations. Therefore, preschools, schools, parents and child groups are the earliest and the best places to start the inclusionary process, a process that will continue into the community at large. It is also critical to continue to see sensible changes across industries, especially those who target children, like fashion and toys, as they provide opportunities to develop the much-desired qualities of compassion, empathy, and helpfulness. It can teach us and our children that the greater the diversity, the richer our capacity to create a more humane, inclusive, and respective society.

In this chapter I showcased a sample of the many inspiring stories that turned the tide on inclusion. The transformations that the fashion industry, fashion media, toy companies, and even individuals like Talia and Donte have led helped the concept of social inclusion become a more operational one. We see from their stories, motivated by their growth mindsets, how promoting an inspirational yet realistic set of measures can gear toward a society for all. It is true that with a growth mindset, change can commence any time, but it is also true that if we essentially target to constructively interrupt our younger generation, who are the most susceptible to change, this will sustain the promotion of social integration at the earliest and help foster inclusive societies.

Learning that the individual drive for change and impact on social inclusion is as important as the collective businesses and industrial changes, we must start taking responsibility for disrupting what we have known to be normal to ensure inclusion. Let us act by questioning the norms, moving from a fixed *"this is how it is"* mindset to a growth *"we can change"* mindset and challenge our own perspectives. We can all endorse an inclusive world by doing our bit for society and opening our eyes and minds to possible small adaptations or big transformations. At the end of the day, regardless of our differences, people are people, and when everyone is included, everyone wins.

In the last chapter, I will be talking more about how **Inclusion starts with U** and conclude with some take-aways that I hope will inspire you to kick off your own journey for promoting inclusion.

12

WHY INCLUSION STARTS WITH YU

The truth of the matter is the initial intention of writing **Inclusion starts with YU** was self-seeking. It was about sharing with the world my own experience of self-discovery, the journey of self-reflecting, the struggle in learning who I was and what I wanted in life, and the even bigger struggle of not acknowledging that what I wanted was different from the norm or peoples' expectations of what is considered the norm.

I knew in my heart that I wanted to be a full person, an ambitious, confident, self-fulfilled individual who does not want to define herself by the socially conditioned sense of duties. I wanted more. I wanted to dream big and achieve big. Yet, regardless of what I knew, my journey, like the journeys of many others, began by trying to take the easier route of being "normal," regardless of the mental frustration and discomfort that it brought. I hid my true passions and ambitions to fit in and reconsidered the excitement that new opportunities brought or dreams I dared to dream. I apologized for wanting to work, travel, expand my horizon, learn, develop, and achieve. I departed on a journey of self-destruction, I must say, a journey driven entirely by the need to hide my differences and the fear of acknowledging that I am different. It all came with the distress of paying the social cost of being different—the cost of exclusion.

It was only when I embarked on the journey of discovering Diversity and Inclusion within the professional context—accompanied by my individual curiosity—that I realized that the struggles of being different were common and exclusion was a common terminology known in the world of diversity. It was felt and measured across every aspect of society and focused beyond the visible diversity traits like gender, race, generation, age, physical abilities, and body types to include the invisible traits like background, work style, sexual orientation, communication style, mindset, behavior, aspirations, and much more. My fears were not unusual nor out of place. Digging deeper, I learned that the issue stems from the fact that our world is not yet an inclusive world, not fully ready to accept differences nor treat people fairly and with respect for who they really are, regardless of their diversities. Not everyone is open to giving equal opportunity to others, or is willing to support the unique and nontraditional setups of needs of individuals. Many things around us are still not designed to encourage inclusion, biases still exist in the way we think and how we behave, and cultural evolution and mindset change are still moving at a snail's pace when it comes to promoting inclusion. All in all, people are not yet fully ready to set differences aside and see people as unique individuals, and accept that everyone is different—different just like us.

Like the luminary individuals who have realized this about the world earlier than I did and have taken actions to inspire change, I have seen the benefit of investing in the same purpose through **Inclusion starts with U.**

I looked to touch upon numerous personal and professional topics to help individuals realize the true term of Diversity and Inclusion and encourage them to join the conversation. Being an HR professional, my ambition was also to promote the importance of the D&I philosophy to business leaders and professionals within the corporate world and help build a culture of inclusion within organizations. Additionally, my aim was to promote inclusion personally within our societies and to inspire people to help me move the needle on D&I.

I wrote *Inclusion Starts with U* for all those who, like me, have struggled or are still struggling with their own differences, for every person who still feels judged, ignored, labeled, or excluded because of their uniqueness. My determination lies in motivating them to embrace their own differences, turn them into advantages, and realize how amazing individuals can be by bringing those differences to the table. Like me, I wanted them to experience, by overcoming their fears, how one day it will just click, one day they will realize what is important and what is not, and they will learn to care less about what other people think and care more about what they think of themselves. They will realize how far they have come, and they will just smile. They will smile because, like me, they will feel truly proud of themselves and the people they have fought to become. They will be stronger, bolder, and more daring to live their own lives on their own, within their own values.

Throughout my career it has not been unusual for me to be the only woman in the room. This has sometimes posed challenges, but also created opportunities for me to develop as a person and as a professional and rise as a leader in the Diversity and Inclusion space. It is true that I am not a sociologist, nor a psychologist, but within both the HR and D&I spaces, I have seen firsthand the opportunity that comes from embracing different perspectives and seeing differences as a chance to grow. I have seen the benefits of bringing D&I to the forefront of the business world and accordingly decided to emphasize through **Inclusion starts with U** how both businesses and individuals have that transformative power to achieve through PBM (policy, mindset, and behavior) a more open, diverse, and inclusive society.

As a starting point, we need to remember how critical it is to intentionally invest in diversity in the workplace and be serious about bringing those diverse teams into the organization. It is important to ensure diversity in our hiring processes, promotions, and retention of our diverse talent who will bring their own perspectives, ideas, skills, and practices to help create organizations that can outperform others. While diversity ignites creativity, problem-solving, and innovation, we have seen in this book that this matters little unless inclusion is promoted too. A company's workforce may be diverse, but if people do not feel safe, welcomed, respected, and valued, the company would not be inclusive nor will it perform to its highest potential.

There is mounting evidence to prove that in order to win, we must create an inclusive workplace where people can collaborate and share their thoughts without fear of judgment or punishment. Inclusion drives belonging, purpose, and engagement, and it can be fortified by revisiting all internal policies and principles with attention to discrimination. In the workplace and from a policy perspective, it is essential to deploy Flex @ work and family-friendly policies which were not universally applicable arrangements, but now an unexpected and unprecedented pandemic has changed it all. In one swoop, many have been pushed to incorporate those policies to help reflect the reality of our present, and we too should not wait any longer.

Hand in hand with policy validations, it has become vital to highlight the evolving role of women in our organizations. After all, empowering women has become more of a human matter, a widespread priority in closing the gaps and achieving gender balance. Empowerment of women also helps in moving the dial on pay equity and realizing the importance of gender equality and equity in driving inclusion. When it comes to behavioral changes, we need to remember that inclusive leadership and how we behave as leaders have become the hallmark of inclusive leaders. We have opportunities through self-quizzes and assessments to measure our individual inclusiveness and help realize development opportunities on all levels. Let us not forget our conscious and unconscious biases, micro-affirmations, and microaggressions which, as insignificant and innocent as they might seem, can take psychological tolls on people.

Let us make sure to use the techniques shared in this book to help make our own judgment more balanced and help us commit further to Diversity and Inclusion in the way we interact with others. When it comes to the workplace, there is no secret that the benefits of implementing D&I initiatives, as seen in ***Inclusion Starts with I U***, are wide ranging and varied. There is literally no downside. They range from attracting the most qualified employees and creating a happy workforce with high job satisfaction to fostering innovation and greater financial success.

Aside from the transformative power of businesses, we cannot overlook the power of individuals and personal influencers in fostering inclusion. In *Inclusion Starts with I U*, we have underlined how some inspiring individuals have also turned the tide on inclusion without the assistance of major investments or substantial strategies. All it takes is a shift in mindset and a willingness to challenge the norm to gear toward an inclusive society.

Reality is you can do it too. You also can be a pioneer of inclusion. This decade is a moment for you, me, and everyone else to turn beliefs and commitments into action. Start by asking yourselves what small and big actions you can do to invest in purpose. It is about the type of world you want to live in, the choices you make, and the vision you have in order to speed up the building of an equal and inclusive future for everyone. Remember that women and men everywhere are fighting, struggling, and advocating for that inclusive and equal world, and someday they will prevail. The greater the number of people who join their side, the sooner they will prevail.

Let's not stay behind. Let us come together and be more engaged and vocal in promoting the message of a diverse, inclusive, and tolerant society. It is an uphill battle, but peace, prosperity, and advancement depend on it. All it takes is one, one person to care and commit to act. Since you now know it, be the "one" to champion it. After all, inclusion can always start with U.

ABOUT THE AUTHOR
(EXTENDED BIO/CREDENTIALS)

Sarah Tabet is an HR professional with more than a decade of well-rounded multinational experience in the human resources field. She is an inspirational speaker, author and an award-winning and ardent proponent of Diversity and Inclusion. She is committed and passionate about creating winning people strategies, positively driving employee engagement and reinforcing employer and HR brands.

Aside from Sarah's commitment to people and love for HR, she always seeks to develop new skills and continuously improve as a person. She is an entrepreneur, a sports devotee, a pottery enthusiast and has her own blog (www. sarahtabet.com) to help her engage with others on several topics with ambition to continuously expand her knowledge. She holds a bachelor's degree in Finance and a certificate from INSEAD. As a speaker, she has been invited to speak regionally on various topics on the Future of the workplace, HR Digital Transformation, Diversity and Inclusion, HR and Women empowerment and has also been featured in several publications related to HR, personal development and the D&I topics. In January 2020, Sarah was granted the Women in Leadership Award (WIL) for the category of Diversity and Inclusion from the MICE quotient and though this book she continues to promote the message and need for a diverse, inclusive and more tolerant world.